the adopter's handbook

information
resources
services

Amy Neil Salter

Updated by Jenifer Lord

Published by
British Association for Adoption & Fostering
(BAAF)
Saffron House
6–10 Kirby Street
London EC1N 8TS
www.baaf.org.uk

Charity registration 275689 (England and Wales) and SC039337 (Scotland)

© Amy Neil Salter, 2002, 2004, 2006, 2012

British Library Cataloguing in Publication Data
A catalogue record for this book is available from the British Library

ISBN 978 1 907585 39 5

Project management by Shaila Shah, Director of Publications, BAAF

Designed by Helen Joubert Design

Printed in Great Britain by The Lavenham Press

Trade distribution by Turnaround Publisher Services, Unit 3, Olympia Trading Estate, Coburg Road, London N22 6TZ

BAAF is the leading UK-wide membership organisation for all those concerned with adoption, fostering and child care issues.

Contents

Acknowledgements

Several people have helped make this guide what it is. Useful information has been supplied and sections and draft of the guide have been reviewed by many professionals and experienced parents involved in adoption. I am grateful for their input, advice and guidance. Thanks to members of Adoption UK, who completed the initial questionnaire which sparked this process, and to the following people for their comments on parts or all of the original draft: Hedi Argent, Daphne Batty, Miranda Davies, Lynda Gilbert, Gill Haworth, Marion Hundleby, Mary Lane, Jenifer Lord, Philly Morrall, Shaila Shah, John Simmonds and Justin Simon. Katrina Wilson and Florence Merredew supplied helpful information for the second edition.

About the author

Amy Neil Salter has had a personal involvement with adoption and is a freelance medical writer by profession. She is currently a practising psychotherapist at a community mental health centre in the USA.

This book is dedicated to her parents, who taught her everything.

This edition

This edition was updated by Jenifer Lord who was for many years a Child Placement consultant in BAAF's Southern region. She is a member of an adoption and permanence panel and has written several books on adoption for BAAF.

Foreword

Adoption is a mass of contradictions. For every rule, there is an equal and opposite rule. For every practice, there is an exception. For every national statement, there is a local interpretation. What is in the best interests of one child is not in the best interests of another. And adoption services vary from one locality to another, with prospective adopters and adoptive parents being subject to different approaches to adoption. How then is the average prospective adopter or adoptive parent meant to survive, let alone understand, what adoption is all about?

Talking to others who have been through the process is invaluable, for example, through peer support organisations such as Adoption UK, but also reading around the subject is crucial. For that, *The Adopter's Handbook* answers many of the questions that you will have and deals with the seeming contradictions or counter-intuition that adoption sometimes requires.

Since it was first published in 2002, it has helped many of the thousands of parents who adopt each year. It does this by recognising that adoptive families are special and that the process of adoption is special. Of course, all families – birth or adoptive – are special, but adoptive families can have an added dimension to the challenges of parenting children. It doesn't make the family or the parents or the children involved better people or parents, but it does make them different, and it does mean that many of them will need extra support and understanding. It's important to acknowledge that difference, for it has many practical effects and consequences.

The reason for this is the children that lie at the heart of the system. In general, the children who are adopted today are those who have been taken into the local authority care system, many of them having suffered some level of abuse or neglect within their birth families, and many with a range of special needs that have to be met by their adoptive families.

Because of this, there is a knotty tangle of legislation, regulations and guidance designed to protect the best interests of the children awaiting adoption. And so there should be, but for the prospective adopters who put themselves forward to parent these children, it can be a bewildering, slow and highly intrusive process. On top of that, there is a necessary, but complicated, dialogue that must go on between the social work professionals who work in adoption agencies, the courts and the parents who will ultimately care for the children.

Via these hard-working professionals, there is a journey to becoming an adoptive parent during which beliefs and expectations will be challenged. It will be an exhilarating, rewarding and enriching journey, but at times it may also be an infuriating, disheartening and depressing one. *The Adopter's Handbook* is an essential companion for that journey, acting as a clear and authoritative source of information, advice and support.

That a new edition has been published is welcome, not least because of the revisions to the regulations and guidance around adoption that were published in England in 2011, but also because of the continuing importance of adoption for children in care – something that is being crucially highlighted by the current government. There is still a need for adopters to come forward, for the process to be speeded up and for more support to be provided – and *The Adopter's Handbook* is one part of showing why that needs to happen.

As part of that, prospective adopters and adoptive parents need to know how the adoption system works, what to expect and what are their rights and duties. *The Adopter's Handbook* does just that.

Jonathan Pearce, Chief Executive, Adoption UK
November 2011

Introduction

Why a guide?

ADOPTING A CHILD is a "human" process – indeed, a "life" process. It is a process in which adults commit themselves to bringing a child into their home, to love and to nurture, and most importantly, to meet the specific needs of that child. Yet adoption is also a service provided by your local authority or by an adoption agency. As adopters, therefore, you are active participants in that service, and it is in your best interest to know as much as possible about the process of adoption and about the wider issues that may affect you and your family along the way.

The purpose of this guide is to help you to help yourself throughout the adoption process and beyond. So, you may be interested to read this information for any of the following reasons:

Because adoption has changed: Adoption and fostering of children in England, Wales and Scotland has undergone immense change in the last few years and adoption law changed very significantly on 30 December 2005. There has been continuing interest in adoption from the government, the press, and from the parents and professionals involved so closely in the adoption process. There is, consequently, a need for accurate, precise information about adoption *before, during* and *after* the "big" event.

Because being informed and aware helps avoid misunderstandings and needless stress: If you know what to expect along the way – for example, the expectations of social workers, the length of time involved, and the potential needs of the child – you will be better able to handle the potential ups and downs of the adoption experience. "Forewarned is forearmed" has never been more true than with adoption – the more you know, the less likely you are to be "surprised" by various events.

Because you will need support and information throughout the adoption process and beyond: If you're just starting on the road to adoption, you'll find that certain aspects of adoption practice may vary from region to region. Use this guide to give you a general understanding of adoption, while asking your social worker to inform you of specific issues after the adoption – when the initial joys of adopting a child have receded and the parents suddenly are left with "real life" issues to face. Use this guide to point yourself in the right direction to find the information and services that can help you build your own framework of support – as much or as little as you need.

Because you want to help your child: During and after adoption, you may suddenly find you need information from a variety of sources – medical, psychological and educational, for instance. You suddenly need to become "expert" in many areas and need to know how to access the systems and services available to you. There is a wealth of information available. The purpose of this guide is to present it between two covers, so you can seek appropriate information and access to services quickly and easily.

Because you are a "consumer" of adoption services: It is, therefore, in your best interests to have a general awareness of the laws, regulations and practice guidelines that affect adoption services provided by local authorities and registered voluntary agencies. Knowledge of these will enable you to ensure the service you receive is of the highest possible quality. It will also enable you to take action if you believe you are not receiving an adequate service.

Although you are being assessed throughout most of the adoption process, you must also feel free to express your own opinions and feelings – even when they differ from those of your social worker, local authority or adoption agency. This guide provides details of the adoption services you should expect to receive, your rights throughout the adoption process, and where to find help if you have a question or complaint about these services, rights or procedures.

Who is this guide for?

There are many people involved in the adoption process. If the adoption experience has touched your life in any way, then this guide is for you as well as for:

- **adoptive parents** who adopted years ago, but who continue to confront issues and want to find the best help available for their children;

- **prospective adopters** just beginning the adoption process – use this guide as your "road map" throughout the adoption and, later, as backup information as the adoption proceeds;

- **social care professionals** who want to know what adoptive parents and prospective adopters really think and what they really want to know;

- **anyone adopted as a child** and who is seeking information and support;

- **everyone involved with the issues of adoption** or who interacts with adopted children – teachers, mental health professionals, medical professionals, education authorities.

When you have finished using this guide, pass it on to someone else. The more people who are aware of adoption and the issues involved, the easier it will be for our adopted children to live in a community that understands, and is sensitive to, their needs.

Please note that this guide is primarily for readers in England and Wales as the legislative framework, processes and procedures described here pertain to law in England and Wales. However, in many cases, resources throughout the UK are listed, i.e. organisations and support networks in England, Wales, Scotland and some in Northern Ireland. We hope that this will be helpful to our readers.

How to use this guide

This guide is divided into five sections, based on *topics identified by adoptive parents.* Each section is organised according to questions adopters commonly ask. Each section also includes the following standard features:

- **A list of specific topics** covered in the section: this gives you a brief overview of the section so you may determine if it contains the information you're seeking;

- **Terms you may need to know** that are used in adoption, and may be unfamiliar;

- **Helpful resources:** books, information, organisations and services that can help you to help yourself in meeting your and your child's needs;

- Also included are **brief descriptions of current programmes, new initiatives, services and legislation** that enable you to be an informed "consumer" of adoption services. This information is not intended to provide a basis for antagonism. It is provided in the spirit of "informed co-operation" – to enable you to work co-operatively with everyone involved in the adoption process.

In addition, this guide includes three **appendices** for quick, easy access to books and magazines (Appendix 1); the useful organisations and resources mentioned in each section (Appendix 2); and relevant sections from the 2011 National Minimum Standards for adoption and statutory Adoption Guidance for England which have been alluded to frequently (Appendix 3). Lastly, an **index** helps you look up particular topics quickly.

The information in each section is presented in a *quick reference format,* so you can:

- look up information when you need it – there is no need to read the entire guide at once; and

- look for information to meet your specific needs – all children and families differ, so your concerns and needs will also differ. There is no need to read through information that does not apply to you.

This fourth edition has been comprehensively updated. It includes information from the Adoption Agencies and Independent Review of Determinations (Amendment) Regulations 2011, the Adoption: National Minimum Standards (NMS) 2011, and the revised Adoption Guidance 2011 for England.

Note: We have done our best to ensure that details for the organisations listed are correct. However, as we all know, organisations move, change their names, or even close down. Thankfully, the internet makes checking and tracking down services much easier than before; most of the organisations listed now have websites, which they didn't when the guide was first published.

Adoption: your questions answered

1

In this section:

→ gain an overview of the adoption process and of the points to consider before proceeding with adoption

→ discover how the adoption process works and how to work effectively with everyone involved in that process

→ find out who can or cannot adopt and what factors are important

→ learn about intercountry adoption and about specific issues that may affect this

The children

In the UK, there are currently around 88,000 children looked after by local authorities. Numbers have risen steadily over the last few years. Being "in care" or being "looked after" means that most of these children are not living with their birth parent/s, but are living in foster care or in community homes. Many of these children will eventually return to their birth family, some of them after a relatively short time. However, some of these children are waiting to be adopted. In recent years, around 5,200 children have been adopted annually, of whom almost three-quarters, or 3,790 children, were looked after, i.e. in the care of the local authority.

All sorts of children need adoption. These include infants, toddlers and school-age children; groups of brothers and sisters who want to stay together; disabled children; children with learning disabilities; children from different minority ethnic communities – all these children can benefit tremendously from family life. We estimate that there are currently about 4,000 children waiting to be adopted.

Although it is in the child's – and everyone's – best interests to remain with his or her birth family whenever possible, adoption may be recommended as one of a range of options for permanence when the child's welfare is considered to be at risk if the child returns to or remains with the birth family.

The European Court of Human Rights considers the relationship between birth parent/s and child to be 'a fundamental aspect of family life that is not terminated when a child is placed in care'. A local authority's decision to remove a child from the birth family must, therefore, be based on reasons that comply with the European Convention on Human Rights.

How does a child come to need to be adopted?

Figure 1 shows the general process by which children become looked after by a local authority and may be placed for adoption. A general knowledge of this process can help adoptive parents understand the experiences of their child becoming looked after, the time periods involved in each stage of the process, and the attempts by local authorities to rehabilitate the child with the birth family.

When is foster care, rather than adoption, considered best for a child?

Children's services departments will consider long-term fostering, a residence order or a special guardianship order for a child if it believes the child will benefit from continued involvement with the birth family, or if the child is older and does not wish to be adopted. In some cases, a child's sense of identity and self-esteem may be strongly connected to the birth family, but his or her additional needs require that he or she be fostered or cared for under a residence order or a special guardianship order. Long-term foster arrangements, residence orders or special guardianship orders may also be considered if the child's birth parents are able and willing to continue to exercise some degree of parental responsibility for the child.

Adoption is considered for the child if the local authority has assessed that the child's needs – physical, emotional and developmental – cannot be met by the birth parents or by other family members. In order for these needs to be met, the child needs to be placed in a new family that is in a legal position to commit themselves to the child emotionally, socially and legally throughout childhood and beyond as the child's legal parents.

Figure 1 **Routes by which a child becomes looked after and potentially is placed for adoption**

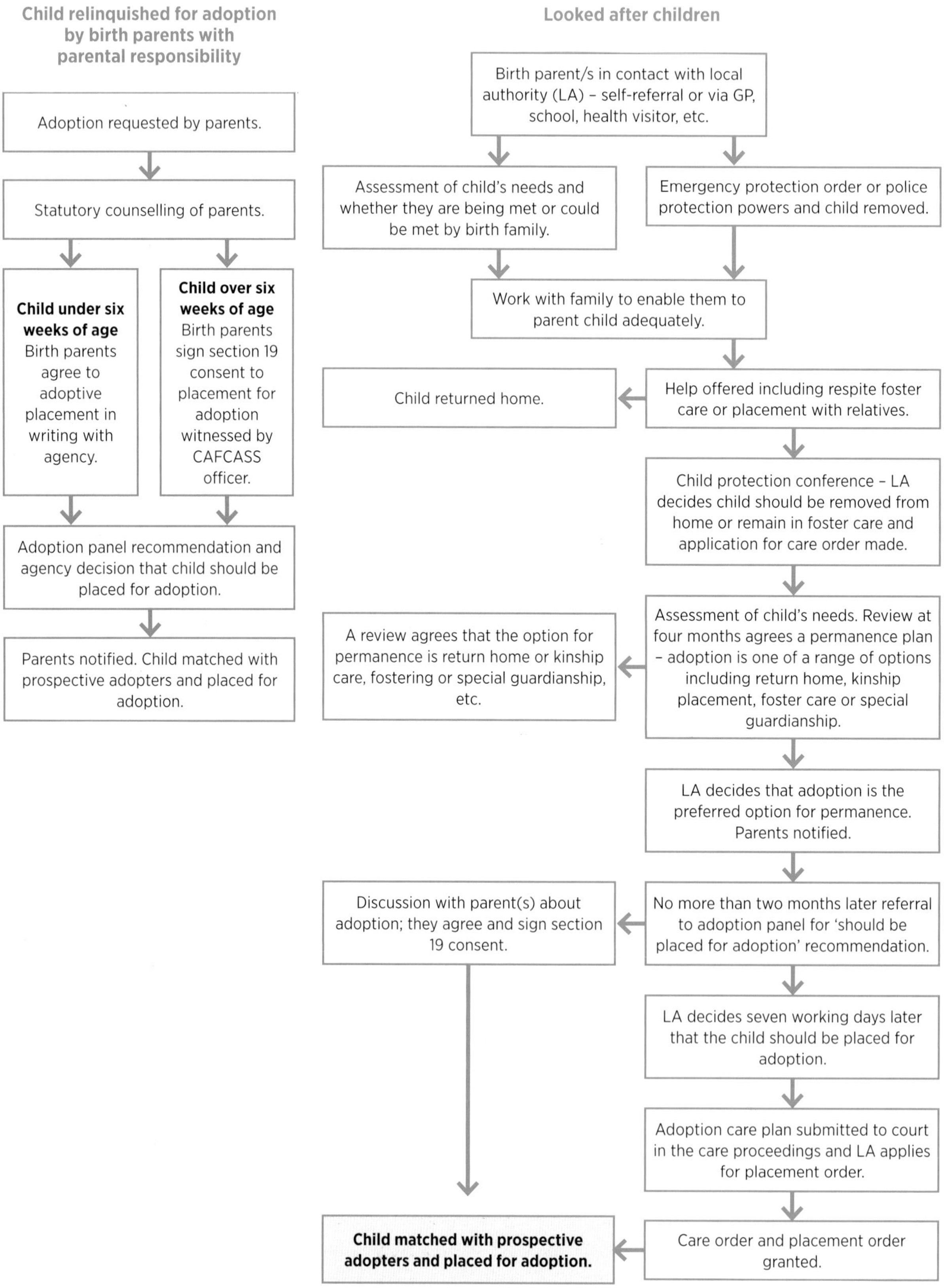

Child relinquished for adoption by birth parents with parental responsibility

Looked after children

Adoption requested by parents.

⬇

Statutory counselling of parents.

⬇

Child under six weeks of age
Birth parents agree to adoptive placement in writing with agency.

Child over six weeks of age
Birth parents sign section 19 consent to placement for adoption witnessed by CAFCASS officer.

⬇

Adoption panel recommendation and agency decision that child should be placed for adoption.

⬇

Parents notified. Child matched with prospective adopters and placed for adoption.

Birth parent/s in contact with local authority (LA) – self-referral or via GP, school, health visitor, etc.

⬇

Assessment of child's needs and whether they are being met or could be met by birth family.

Emergency protection order or police protection powers and child removed.

⬇

Work with family to enable them to parent child adequately.

⬇

Child returned home. ⬅ Help offered including respite foster care or placement with relatives.

⬇

Child protection conference – LA decides child should be removed from home or remain in foster care and application for care order made.

⬇

A review agrees that the option for permanence is return home or kinship care, fostering or special guardianship, etc. ⬅ Assessment of child's needs. Review at four months agrees a permanence plan – adoption is one of a range of options including return home, kinship placement, foster care or special guardianship.

⬇

LA decides that adoption is the preferred option for permanence. Parents notified.

⬇

Discussion with parent(s) about adoption; they agree and sign section 19 consent. ⬅ No more than two months later referral to adoption panel for 'should be placed for adoption' recommendation.

⬇

LA decides seven working days later that the child should be placed for adoption.

⬇

Adoption care plan submitted to court in the care proceedings and LA applies for placement order.

⬇

Child matched with prospective adopters and placed for adoption. ⬅ Care order and placement order granted.

Reproduced (with amendments) from *Effective Adoption Panels,* 5th edn., BAAF, 2012 (forthcoming).

Is adoption right for you?

'... it will be important for all concerned to be realistic in recognising that long-term and persistent trauma can result in behaviours that are both challenging to live with and resistant to change.'
S. Byrne, *Linking and Introductions*, BAAF, 2000

Clearly, there are many children who need a loving and secure home, and many more people are needed to be adoptive parents. But this doesn't *necessarily* mean adoption is the right choice for everyone. It is important to consider in a clear and logical manner your decision to adopt – to avoid the temptation to be led to your decision purely by emotion.

The fact that you are reading this guide means you are investigating the option of adopting children. You and your family may have discussed many of the different issues involved already. But if you don't know much about adoption, or don't know anyone who has adopted children, you might want to think about some of the following questions.

Why do I/we want to adopt?

We cannot escape the fact that deciding to have children, through birth or through adoption, fulfils some of our own needs and desires to become parents and to raise a family. After all, this is a natural process in life. Yet most children waiting for adoption have specific emotional and physical needs (see Section 4 for more explanation) and require parents who can commit to being with them through good times and through tough times. The process of adoption, therefore, must necessarily focus on the *child's* needs and on meeting those needs as much as possible.

When you begin the process of adoption, you must also be willing to address your own emotional needs (for example, attachment issues from your own childhood, infertility issues, grief over a lost child, etc.) and must be sure that adoption is not simply a route to overcome your own difficulties.

Is parenting an adopted child different from parenting my own birth child?

Yes. Most children who are placed for adoption have experienced some degree of abuse and/or neglect. And all children needing adoption suffer the trauma of separation from, and loss of, their birth family. These events affect children of *all* ages (even infants) and in many different ways (see Section 4 for more information about these effects). While most children are able to "recover" from their experiences when placed in a loving environment, it is important to understand that the road to recovery can be difficult and frustrating for both the child and the adoptive parents.

It is also important to understand that older children (age 3+), especially, will have begun to develop their own personality and habits by the time they are adopted. As parents, your personality and habits will still influence the child, but less so than if the child had been born to you.

Is it "easier" to parent an older child or a younger child?

Research* has shown that infant adoptions are generally successful for both the child and the parents. Yet, there is no guarantee that a younger child will have fewer difficulties than an older child. Even babies can suffer the effects of early trauma or neglect (see Section 4). Only you can decide what age child you want to adopt. The most important consideration is to determine how you can best meet the needs of that child.

Can children who have experienced trauma, abuse and/or neglect ever overcome these experiences?

Yes. Section 4 of this guide describes the many complex emotional, developmental and physical difficulties children can experience as a result of abuse and/or neglect. In some cases, such experiences can affect the physical growth and development of neural connections in the brain and thus affect the child's emotions and behaviour. Studies[†] have shown that, with appropriate treatment (medical, psychiatric and/or psychological), these neural connections can form – the brain can be helped to adapt to compensate for earlier neglect.

When considering adoption, the two key things to remember are:

- providing a loving and secure home will help the child, but may not help the child resolve *all* of his or her problems – you may have to seek additional assistance from a variety of sources; and

- the wounds of abuse and neglect run deep – even if the child was removed from the abusive environment at an early age.

As adoptive parents, therefore, we must look realistically at our own expectations of our child and his or her "recovery". It may take many years (perhaps a lifetime) for the child to overcome the complex effects of early trauma.

How does the adoption process work?

Once you have decided you are interested in adopting a child, the first step is to contact a local authority's adoption team or a voluntary adoption agency to ask for information and procedures.

---

* C. Sellick, J. Thoburn, T. Philpot, *What works in adoption and foster care?*, Barnardo's/ BAAF, 2004
† J. Selwyn, W. Sturgess, D. Quinton and C. Baxter, *Costs and Outcomes of Non-Infant Adoptions*, BAAF, 2006; B. Perry, *Maltreated Children: Experience, brain development and the next generation*, W.W. Norton, New York, 1995

HELPFUL BOOKS

For more information and publications about the effects of early trauma, see Section 4 and Appendix 1 of this guide.

Attachment, Trauma and Resilience: Therapeutic caring for children
by Kate Cairns, BAAF, 2002
Written by someone who fostered several children over a 25-year period, this book provides an illustration of family life with children who had lived through overwhelming stress and how they were helped to overcome it.

First Steps in Parenting the Child Who Hurts: Tiddlers and toddlers by Caroline Archer, Jessica Kingsley, 1999
This book approaches the attachment and developmental issues that arise when even the youngest child is in your care.

Next Steps in Parenting the Child Who Hurts: Tykes and teens by Caroline Archer, Jessica Kingsley, 1999
This book follows on logically from the *First Steps* book and continues into the challenging journey through childhood and into adolescence.

The Primal Wound: Understanding the adopted child by Nancy Verrier, BAAF, 2009 (UK edn)
This book contains profound insights and revelations on what being adopted means to adopted people. The book explores the "primal wound" that results when a child is separated from his or her mother and the trauma it can cause.

Coming Home to Self: Healing the primal wound by Nancy Verrier, BAAF, 2010 (UK edn)
Considers the effects of separation trauma on brain development and explores some of the most troubling emotions and examines ways of healing and achieving meaningful relationships and personal power.

Loving and Living with Traumatised children by Megan Hirst, BAAF, 2005
Looks at the experience of adopting traumatised children and the effects this can have on their carers and adoptive parents, based on the experiences of nine individuals.

If you are interested in adopting a specific child you have seen in a family-finding publication or website: you should contact the organisation that produces the publication/website for information and then the local authority looking after the child.

When you contact an adoption agency: you will receive written information which Standard 10.3 (of the National Minimum Standards 2011) specifies should be within five working days of your enquiry. You will then be offered a follow-up interview with a social worker and/or an invitation to an information meeting. This will give you the opportunity to find out more about adoption and about the waiting children, to ask questions and to talk a bit about your hopes and plans. This should happen within two months of your initial enquiry. If, after this, you and the agency decide to proceed, they will give you an application form to complete and return. You will be asked at this stage for permission to carry out checks which the agency is required to make.

The key players

There are five key players in the adoption process:

- the child;

- the local authority adoption team OR the voluntary adoption agency which has assessed you, your assessing social worker and team manager;

- the local authority which is responsible for the child (which may or may not be the same one as above), the child's social worker and team manager;

- you, the prospective adoptive parent/s; and

- the birth parent(s) or child's legal guardians.

The courts also play a role in the adoption process, at different points along the way.

Voluntary adoption agencies

Voluntary adoption agencies are usually smaller agencies than local authorities. They work to the same regulations, guidance and national minimum standards as local authorities. They recruit, assess, approve and support adoptive parents who will have children looked after by a local authority placed with them.

Social workers

All social workers in the UK are required to have a qualification approved by the GSCC or equivalent body. They are required to be registered with these bodies. The qualification involves a minimum of three years' training, culminating in a degree.

The following organisations are involved in the development and management of the social care industry:

- **General Social Care Council** (GSCC)

- **Ofsted** (Office for Standards in Education, Children's Services and Skills)

- **Department for Education** (DfE)

- **Social Care Institute for Excellence** (SCIE) collects and synthesises up-to-date knowledge about what works in social care and makes that widely available.

National Minimum Standards are in force to specify how adoption and fostering services should be delivered. Adoption services are inspected every three years against these Standards (see Appendix 3). The DfE publishes guidance – statutory and practice guidance – which shapes the way that adoption and fostering services are provided.

Figure 2 shows a *general* flowchart of the route to adoption of a child, as seen by the local authority. Below, we look in detail at the adoption process for prospective adopters.

Figure 2 **Process for identifying a family after a decision that a child should be placed for adoption**

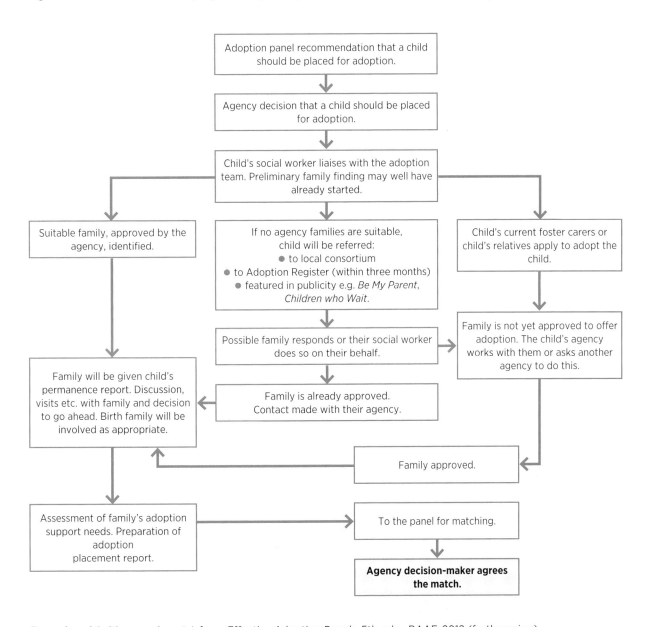

Reproduced (with amendments) from *Effective Adoption Panels*, 5th edn., BAAF, 2012 (forthcoming).

How can I prepare for adoption?

No one can ever be fully "prepared" for the adoption process and for the eventual arrival of a child in their home. But there are things you can do to make the process a bit easier and to "initially" prepare yourself as much as possible to meet the needs of the child who may become a part of your family.

- Once you tell an agency about your interest in adoption, you will be given written and verbal information. When you have applied to the agency you will be given preparation, which may be by attendance at groups. You will have a chance to explore a range of issues about adoption and children's needs. You can read *Preparing to Adopt* (the Workbook), part of a training guide published by BAAF in 2010 (3rd edn) and watch the DVD that accompanies it (Appendix 1).

- You can read about the adoption process, so you understand the functions and responsibilities of everyone involved – this helps avoid misunderstandings. *Adopting a Child*, a popular guide published by BAAF and regularly revised (most recently in February 2011), provides a comprehensive account.

- You can gain experience of other people's children, e.g. attend Parentcraft classes at your local clinic or hospital, or volunteer to help at your local school, play group or nursery.

- You can meet adoptive parents, through joining Adoption UK.

- If you are a lesbian or gay adopter, you can meet others through joining New Family Social.

- You can read about and be aware of the impact of trauma and neglect on children of all ages.

- You can read about the experiences of others who have adopted (see booklist).

- You can read about adoption law from the perspective of adopters in *Adoption Law for Adopters*, published by Adoption UK in January 2006.

It is impossible to prepare yourself for every aspect of the adoption process, because you can't anticipate everything that may occur. The best preparation is to read about the adoption process and about the children as you go along, so you will know how to access help right away, if you need it.

Who can adopt?

Almost anyone can apply to be an adoptive parent if they can show that they can provide a loving, secure home that will meet the needs of a particular child.

Adoption Guidance makes clear that no one can be denied the opportunity to be considered as an adoptive parent because of ethnic background, marital status, sexuality or age. It spells out the eligibility criteria:

- The prospective adopter(s) is single, married, in a civil partnership or an unmarried couple (same sex or opposite sex) and 21 years old. (The birth parent in a step-parent adoption must be 18 or older.)

HELPFUL ORGANISATIONS

General information about adoption

Adoption UK
A UK-wide support organisation for adoptive parents and prospective adopters with local groups and messageboards. Also publishes a monthly magazine, *Adoption Today*, with news, views and features, and a supplement, *Children Who Wait*, which features children needing adoption.

55 The Green, South Bar Street,
Banbury, Oxfordshire OX16 9AB
Helpline: 0870 770 0450
Tel: 01295 752240
Email: admin@adoptionuk.org.uk
www.adoptionuk.org.uk

British Association for Adoption & Fostering (BAAF)
Has offices throughout the UK and provides up-to-date information about all aspects of adoption, including information about adoption agencies and answers to general questions about adoption. Also publishes useful pamphlets and guides including *Adopting a Child*, and runs a family-finding service, *Be My Parent*, which features waiting children, both in print and online.

Also manages the Adoption Register for England and Wales for the DfE.

Saffron House, 6–10 Kirby Street,
London EC1N 8TS
Tel: 020 7421 2600
www.baaf.org.uk
www.bemyparent.org.uk

Department for Education
The government department responsible for adoption and fostering services and for other services to children and families.

Tel: 0370 000 2288
www.education.gov.uk/adoption

New Family Social is a UK charity for lesbian, gay, bisexual and transgender adopters, foster carers and their children. It provides advice and information, a vibrant messageboard, as well as social events for parents and children to get together.

PO Box 66244
London E9 9BD
Tel: 0843 289 9457
www.newfamilysocial.co.uk

- The prospective adopter or one of them has their permanent home (domicile) in England, Wales, Scotland, Northern Ireland, the Channel Islands, on the Isle of Man, or both members of a couple have been habitually resident there for at least a year before they apply to court for an adoption order.

- Neither prospective adopter nor an adult member of their household has been convicted or cautioned for a specified offence. These are principally offences against children.

Must we have a "normal" family structure in order to apply to adopt children?

A "normal" family structure is impossible to define. You are *not* prohibited from adopting if you live in a family structure that is different from the majority of the population. In fact, research* has found that some family structures, such as single parents, can better meet the needs of particular children (such as those who have been sexually abused or who may need to interact with only one parent).

Couples who live together, as well as married or civil registered couples, can adopt jointly.

We should keep in mind that children may have fewer "predetermined" views of a "normal" or "perfect" family.

Here are some answers to common questions prospective adopters ask regarding family structure.

We are long-term foster carers and we want to adopt our foster child. How do we do this? If you have fostered a child for at least one year, or longer, you can apply to the court for an adoption order, whether or not the child's local authority agrees. However, you must give notice in writing to the local authority three months before you make the application. You can apply much sooner with the agreement of the local authority and it is best to discuss your wishes with the local authority and, if possible, to go through the adoption process with them.

We want to adopt our grandchildren. How can we do this? As relatives of the children, whether or not they are looked after by the local authority, you can apply to adopt them after the children have lived with you for three years. You can apply to the court for permission to apply sooner than this. You must give written notice to the local authority at least three months before you apply for the adoption order. The court will decide if the adoption order or any other order, such as a residence order or a special guardianship order, is in the children's best interests. The court will take into account the local authority's views about this.

---

* See M. Owen, *Novices, Old Hands and Professionals: Adoption by single people,* BAAF, 1999.

HELPFUL BOOKS

Approaching Fatherhood: A guide for adoptive dads by Paul May, BAAF, 2005
The first book in the UK to combine adoptive fathers' experiences with a guide to the adoption process, from the man's point of view.

Becoming Dads by Pablo Fernández, BAAF, 2011
A diarised narrative account of how Pablo and Mike adopt their son.

Flying Solo by Julia Wise, BAAF, 2007
A single parent's adoption story.

Is it True you have Two Mums? by Ruby Clay, BAAF, 2011
Charts the adoption journey of a lesbian couple who adopt three girls.

Looking After our Own: The stories of black and Asian adopters edited by Hope Massiah, BAAF, 2005
Stories from a number of black and Asian adopters about their adoption experiences.

Loving and Living with Traumatised Children: Reflections by adoptive parents by Megan Hirst, BAAF, 2004
A group of adopters tell of their experiences and the effect on themselves of adopting traumatised children.

Novices, Old Hands and Professionals: Adoption by single people by Morag Owen, BAAF, 1999
Documents and comments on the experiences of single adopters and their children.

The Pink Guide to Adoption for Lesbians and Gay Men by Nicola Hill, BAAF, 2009
A step-by-step guide to adopting, including accounts by those going through the process.

My husband and I are from different ethnic backgrounds. Will this affect our ability to adopt a child? In fact, there are many children of mixed ethnic backgrounds, so families such as yours are particularly needed.

My partner and I are not married, but we want to adopt a child. Can we do this? Yes. Unmarried couples (lesbian, gay, or heterosexual) or couples who have not entered into a civil partnership, can adopt jointly.

My partner and I are in a same-sex relationship. Can we adopt a child? Yes. Lesbian or gay couples can adopt jointly just as any other couple.

I am a single parent. Can I adopt a child? Yes, single people can adopt. Research has found that some children benefit from placement with a single adult; for example, girls who have been sexually abused, and children who have witnessed severe conflict between parents or those who will benefit from the one-to-one attention and care provided by one adult.

I am in my late 40s and my partner is over 50. Can we adopt? Yes, this could be possible. Adoption Guidance states that older and more experienced adopters could have something special to offer to older children if they enjoy sufficient health and vigour to meet the child's varied demands; it cautions that too large an age gap between adopter and child may have an adverse effect upon the child. Adopters need to be able to meet the many and varied demands of children in their growing years and be there for them into adulthood.

If we had a placement that disrupted, can we apply for adoption again? If you have previously had a child placed with you for adoption and the placement did not work out for you, don't be put off. The adoption agency which originally approved you must undertake a review of your approval. They must ask their panel to make a recommendation about your continued approval, if the agency is of the view that your approval should be terminated. If the agency proposal is to terminate your approval, you can apply to the Independent Review Mechanism (IRM) for a review of that proposal.

A detailed look at the process for adopters

Ten stops to assessment

After you have applied to adopt, the main steps of the adoption process for prospective adopters are:

1 You attend preparation sessions.

2 Checks, references and a medical are arranged and carried out.

3 A social worker carries out an assessment (also called "home study").

4 The report written by your social worker about you – the Prospective Adopter's Report – is given to an adoption panel for their recommendation of your approval as prospective adopters. The agency makes the final decision.

5 If you are approved, the social workers consider a match between you and a child who has been authorised for adoption by a placement order or a section 19 parental consent. The social worker from the child's agency sends you the Child's Permanence Report and arranges to meet you to discuss the proposed match. If it is agreed that the match will proceed, the child's agency must assess your and the child's support needs and agree a support plan with you.

6   An adoption panel considers the proposed match, makes a recommendation and advises on contact, adoption support and exercise of parental responsibilities. The child's local authority then makes a decision to proceed with the match.

7   You and the child are introduced.

8   The child moves in (i.e. is placed with you).

9   An adoption order is made through the court.

10   You can request an assessment of your post-adoption support needs.

Let's look at each of these steps in detail.

1   Attendance at preparation sessions

All adoption agencies are required to provide preparation and you will almost certainly be invited to a series of group meetings, often about six, of two to three hours each. You will be with other prospective adopters, usually about eight or ten people. As well as hearing from social workers about adoption and the children waiting, you will usually also hear from experienced adopters, an adopted adult and perhaps from a birth parent whose child has been adopted, about their experiences. You will have the opportunity to ask questions and to reflect on your own life experiences and on the impact of any adopted child on your family and how you will adapt to meet their needs.

2   Checks, references and a medical are carried out

This will probably happen over the period that you attend the preparation group and have your assessment. Checks are made of criminal records for you and members of your household aged over 18. Offences other than specified ones, i.e. those against children, need not rule you out, although the nature of the offence and how long ago it occurred will need to be carefully considered. It's vital that you are open and honest. Any attempt at deception will be taken very seriously. Checks will also be made of the local authority where you live. You will be asked for the names of at least three personal referees, people who know you really well, and they will be interviewed. If you have parented children with a previous partner, the agency will want your permission to contact him or her. They may want to talk to adult children whom you've parented. They will want to check that you are not seriously in debt and that payments on your home are up to date. Finally, you will need a full medical examination carried out by your GP. This will be considered by the adoption agency's medical adviser.

3   A social worker carries out an assessment (home study)

The "assessment" or "home study" is a period of several months when the social worker designated to work with you visits you at your home.

HELPFUL BOOKS

Adopting a Child by Jenifer Lord, BAAF, 2011
This popular guide describes what adoption means and how to go about it, including procedures and practices, legal requirements and the costs involved. It includes a list of agencies – local authority and voluntary – throughout the UK (see Appendix 1).

An Adoption Diary by Maria James, BAAF, 2006
A true story of an adoption which tracks Maria's and Rob's journey to adopting a two-year-old child, chronicling the highs and lows along the way.

Checklist for Prospective Adopters, available from Adoption UK (see Appendix 2), lists a variety of questions prospective adopters should consider and should discuss with their social worker at all stages of the adoption process.

Guiding you Through the Adoption Process available from Adoption UK, last revised in 2009
Provides a comprehensive step-by-step guide through the adoption process.

The purpose of these visits is for the social worker to gain a detailed view of you and other family members in the home, in order to assess your suitability to adopt a child.

The length of time for the home study to be completed is determined by the agency, according to its own policies, procedures and workload. However, the statutory Adoption Guidance 2011 sets a standard of eight months between your formal application for approval and presentation to panel for a recommendation for approval.

The social worker records information on the Prospective Adopter's Report. The Prospective Adopter's Report will include a summary of the medical information about you from your GP.

Working effectively with your social worker

The goal of home visits is to assess whether you are suitable to adopt and prepare you for it. Although you may feel uneasy and think the questioning and form-filling too intrusive and detailed, it is best to try to approach these visits with a relaxed, informal attitude. Open, honest communication throughout the home visits will help your social worker provide accurate information to the adoption panel. Remember that the social worker needs to ensure not only your parenting skills and capacity, and match these against a particular child or children, but also that any prospective adopter meets the legal requirements (see Section 2).

Why do adoptive parents have to be "assessed" for parenthood, when people giving birth do not? Simply because the purpose of adoption is to focus on the needs of a particular child who has had to be separated from his or her birth family – a child who is already born, with his or her own developing personality, habits and physical and emotional needs. The task of parenting a child not born to you is different and needs to be recognised as such. The social worker's role is to ensure the child's needs are matched as closely as possible to parents who can meet those needs.

YOUR RIGHTS DURING THE ASSESSMENT PROCESS

The Adoption Guidance 2011 and National Minimum Standards 2011 require that:

- Prospective adopters 'are treated fairly, without prejudice, openly and with respect. They are kept informed, on a regular basis, of the progress (or lack of progress) of their enquiry/application.' NMS 10.2

- 'The adoption panel's recommendations about the suitability of the prospective adopter to adopt a child should be made within eight months of the receipt of the formal application'. Guidance 3.1

You should be given a copy of your Prospective Adopter's Report and you are given ten days to comment upon its contents before the panel meets to consider it.

If you have any questions or concerns during your home study, which you feel unable to discuss with your social worker, or if you have particular difficulties with the assessment process or with your social worker, you can contact your social worker's manager, or the director of the adoption agency. As a last resort you could contact your local Member of Parliament. You may also contact:

Ofsted (Office for Standards in Education, Children's Services and Skills). It has responsibility for the reputation and inspection of all children's services. Adoption and fostering services must be inspected at least three-yearly.

Piccadilly Gate, Store Street
Manchester M1 2WD
Email: enquiries@ofsted.gov.uk
Tel: 0300 123 1231

General Social Care Council, a regulatory body for the social care profession in England that sets national standards, training regulations and social worker registration.

Myson House, Railway Terrace, Rugby CV21 3HT
Tel: 0845 070 0630
www.gscc.org.uk

Equivalent bodies for other countries in the United Kingdom include:

- **Care Council for Wales** www.ccwales.org.uk

- **Northern Ireland Social Care Council (NISCC)** www.niscc.info

- **Scottish Social Services Council (SSSC)** www.sssc.uk.com

4 Your Prospective Adopter's Report is given to an adoption panel

When your home study is completed, your social worker will submit your Prospective Adopters' Report to the local authority or voluntary agency's adoption panel. The **adoption panel** is an advisory group, established by the adoption agency or by the local authority, which:

- considers applications to be approved as adopters (both domestic and intercountry);

- recommends whether or not it believes the prospective applicant/s can meet the needs of a child and, therefore;

- recommends whether or not the applicants should be approved as adoptive parents.

The panel also makes recommendations regarding other aspects of the adoption process, such as whether a child should be placed for adoption and matches between children and adopters. Adoption panels can also advise about support and contact plans and the exercise of parental responsibilities by prospective adopters during placement.

Who is on the adoption panel?

The panel usually consists of about five to ten people, including:

- the Chair – a person who has experience in adoption work and is independent of the agency

- one social worker with experience of adoption

- sometimes a member of the agency's management committee or local authority's social services committee

- usually the medical adviser

- some "independent" persons who are not members or employees of the agency or local authority. Where possible these people should include people with personal experience of adoption.

A panel is only quorate when at least five of its members are present, and this must include the Chair or Vice-chair, a social worker and at least one independent member if the Vice-chair is chairing and not independent.

HELPFUL BOOKS

Effective Adoption Panels (5th edn.) by Jenifer Lord and Deborah Cullen, BAAF, 2012
Primarily aimed at adoption workers and panel members as well as prospective adopters. Full of useful information about the roles and responsibilities of panel members.

Prospective adopters attending adoption panel by Jenifer Lord, BAAF, 2011 (2nd edn.)
Provides guidance for panel members on the prospective adopters' role in a panel meeting, the input they can have, and how their contribution should be evaluated.

Adoption Agencies Regulations require that applicants be invited to attend the panel meeting.

The composition, terms of reference and functions of an adoption panel are set out in the Adoption Agencies Regulations 2005, the Adoption Agencies and Independent Review of Determinations (Amendment) Regulations 2011 and statutory Adoption Guidance 2011.

What issues will the panel consider when considering the application?

The panel will consider the Prospective Adopter's Report provided by your social worker, as well as information about your statutory eligibility and suitability (including marital status, nationality, domicile, criminal records, and financial considerations). Within this context, panel members will focus on the following specific issues.

- **Your reasons for adopting** – panel members will want to be sure that you understand and can address any relevant emotional issues that have led you to adoption.

  For example, the panel will ask: Why have the applicants applied to adopt? Do the applicants understand their motivation to care for a child? Are they able to identify their own needs and expectations regarding adoption? Have they dealt with issues of infertility (if applicable)?

  This is not to say that you must have resolved all such issues, but that you are able to identify and understand them, and to deal with resulting feelings.

- **The child and birth family** – do you understand the intense emotional needs of children (of any age) who have experienced trauma, separation or loss? What are your feelings regarding the birth parents and their inability to care for the child? Will you be ready to deal with needs that are not yet identified in the child?

- **Your family structure** – do you have a support network you can rely on? Are there other children in the family? The child's position in the family can affect his or her ability to adjust to the family and can be affected by the child's particular emotional needs. Also, research has shown that there is a greater risk that the placement will not thrive if the child is placed in a family that has other children close to him or her in age; an age gap of at least two years is usually advisable.*

- **Your relationships** – if you are divorced or have had previous partnerships, panel members will consider whether or not there is a pattern of relationship difficulties that could be repeated in the future and, if so, what plans you would then make for the child.

- **Your age** – while law prohibits discrimination on the basis of age, the panel will want to "maximise" the chances that you will remain fit and healthy well into the child's young adulthood. In order to adopt, you must be at least 21 years old.

- **Your current health** – lifestyle and medical issues will be considered for their impact on you and your family. If you have particular concerns, it is best to talk to your social worker about them.

- **If you have a criminal record** – See *Who Can Adopt?*, p.15.

The panel will also consider issues of culture, "race" and ethnicity; contact with the birth family; financial requirements (e.g. financial support before and after adoption, settling in grants [see Section 2]); and requirements for other adoption support.

5 You are linked and matched with a child

After you have become "approved" prospective adoptive parents, your social worker will begin the process of matching you with a child or children or you can be proactive by looking in *Be My Parent* or *Children Who Wait*. In some cases, a child may have been identified before you began the adoption process (for example, foster carers adopting a foster child; grandparents or other birth relatives adopting a child; or applicants who apply to adopt a specific child).

An adoption agency can only match you with a child who has been "authorised" by the granting of a placement order or the giving of formal consent to placement for adoption by the child's parents (called a section 19 consent).

Your social worker will visit you to discuss the details of a prospective child. If you express an interest in pursuing adoption of the child, the child's social worker and possibly the foster carer/s will also arrange to visit you. You must be given the Child's Permanence Report.

---

* C. Sellick, J. Thoburn, T. Philpot, *What works in adoption and foster care?* Barnardo's/ BAAF, 2004

Your questions answered...

What happens if we're not recommended for approval by the panel?
It is not the panel that will make the final decision but the agency;
the agency is not required to follow the panel's recommendation (see
Figure 2).

**What happens if we're not approved by the local authority or the
agency?** If the agency or local authority proposes not to approve your
application, it must notify you in writing and must give its reasons.
You must also be told if the panel's recommendation was different
from the agency's proposal. You then have 40 days in England and
Wales to make representations to the agency or request a review of
the agency's proposal by the IRM but *not to both* (see below for details
of the IRM). If you do not present your views, the agency can make its
decision. If you make representations to the agency decision maker
within 40 days in England and Wales, he or she may refer you back to
the panel.

If the case is presented again to the panel, the panel must give the
case fresh consideration. Alternatively, the agency may choose (but is
not obligated) to present the case to a different adoption panel (some
agencies have more than one panel, or may present cases to panels of
other agencies). The agency's decision after this second consideration
will then be final.

A final decision can also be made, after considering your views,
without the case going back to panel.

If you are still unhappy about the process, you may use the agency's
representation and complaints procedure.

How long does our "approval" last? Adoption Agencies Regulations
require that the approval should be reviewed at least annually until
a child is placed (at least every two years in Wales) or whenever the
agency considers a review to be necessary. Your agency should give
you clear information about this.

It is important that agency staff have regular contact with approved
adopters who are waiting to be matched with a child. Panels have a
useful role in reviewing the circumstances of waiting adopters and
should receive regular, brief updating reports, perhaps every three or
six months.*

J. Lord and D. Cullen, *Effective Adoption Panels* (5th edn.), BAAF 2012 (forthcoming)

Summary of your rights throughout the approval process

- You must be shown a copy of the social worker's assessment section of the Prospective Adopter's Report (not including the medical information and references).

- You must be given an opportunity of at least ten days to comment on the assessment before it is presented to panel.

- You must be invited to attend the panel meeting.

- If the agency proposes not to approve your application, it must notify you in writing, and give its reasons.

- You must also be told if the panel's recommendation is different from the local authority's or agency's proposal.

- You have 40 days to present your views to the local authority or agency OR to apply to the IRM.

- If you contact the local authority or agency, it then decides whether or not to re-present the case to the panel. It may elect to present the information to a different panel.

- If the same panel considers the case, it must give it *fresh* consideration.

- If you request a review by the IRM, your case will be considered by an IRM panel, which will make a recommendation.

- The local authority or agency's decision after this second consideration will be final.

During these visits, it is important to discuss openly all relevant details about the child. Do not hesitate to ask questions because you fear it might seem "impolite" or "intrusive". After all, you are making a decision that will affect the rest of your life. If you decide not to proceed with a match for a child, you must return the Child's Permanence Report to the agency.

TERMS YOU NEED TO KNOW

The Child's Permanence Report gives detailed information about the child, such as a physical description, his or her background, personality traits and currently known needs – educational, emotional, physical, health and development, etc. The social worker can provide valuable information and insight into the child's history, current relationships and behaviours. Social workers are required to provide the most up-to-date and complete information available.

Independent Review Mechanism (IRM)
Unit 4, Pavilion Business Park
Royds Hall Road
Wortley
Leeds LS12 6AJ
Tel: 0845 450 3956
Email: irm@baaf.org.uk
www.independentreviewmechanism.org.uk

This is an independent review process, conducted by a panel. It is operated by BAAF under contract to the DfE. It applies to cases where an adoption agency in England is proposing not to approve, or to terminate the approval of, adoptive parents. If you receive notification in writing from your adoption agency that it proposes not to approve you, or to terminate your approval as an adoptive parent (this is called a "qualifying determination"), you can apply for a review EITHER to the agency (see above) OR to the IRM, but not to both.

If you decided to apply to the IRM, you must contact the IRM within 40 days of the written notification from the agency. The IRM will arrange for your case to be heard by an independent IRM panel, which you can attend.

The panel will make a recommendation which will go to your agency. The agency will then make the final decision.

Independent Review Mechanism Cymru
7 Cleeve House
Lambourne Crescent
Cardiff CF14 5GP
Tel: 0845 873 1305
Email: irm@irmcymru.org.uk
www.irmcymru.org.uk

This is run by BAAF under contract to the Welsh Assembly Government and is available to people assessed by adoption agencies in Wales. It operates in a very similar way to the IRM in England.

The child's social worker should also discuss contact and support arrangements, the child's need for services after placement and adoption, for example, extra support in school, therapy, etc. There should also be discussion with you about the support that you are likely to need and about the services which the agency will provide, and proposed arrangements for contact (if any).

Adoption Support Services Regulations 2005 and accompanying Guidance came into force on 30 December 2005. These place a duty on local authorities to assess the likely adoption support needs of a child when adoption becomes the plan and to make and agree an adoption support plan with prospective adopters when a potential match is being considered.

HELPFUL PUBLICATIONS/WEBSITES

Resources listing children who are waiting to be adopted

The following publications and websites profile children who need families. If these publications feature a child you are interested in parenting, the child's social worker will still have to make sure that you are the right family for that child.

Be My Parent/www.bemyparent.org.uk

A monthly newspaper and online service produced by BAAF (see Appendix 2) which features photographs and a brief description of children of all ages and backgrounds from all over the UK. The online edition also contains videoclips and enhanced profiles. Available by subscription.

Children Who Wait/www.adoptionuk.org

A listing of children needing new families throughout the UK, updated monthly and also available online. Available by becoming a member of Adoption UK. See Appendix 2 for details on contacting Adoption UK.

Adoption agencies also use **local or specialist media** to feature children needing adoption, e.g. *The Voice*, a weekly aimed at black communities, frequently features black children to attract the interest of black families. Occasionally, for example, during **National Adoption Week** in November, television and national newspapers also alert the public to the needs of children needing adoption and may feature certain children.

A proposed adoption support plan should be discussed with you before the match goes to panel and the proposals for adoption support should be included in the Adoption Placement Report. Once the match has been approved, you and the child's agency should agree the arrangements for the support that the child and you are likely to need after placement and adoption. This could include, for example, financial support, the provision of therapy for the child, support groups or workshops for you, training for you to meet the child's needs, or respite care.

The medical adviser should provide a written health report on each child being considered for adoption. This report should include comments on birth history, family history, past medical history, current physical and mental health and behaviour and, if age appropriate, a developmental assessment. This report should assess the future implications for the child of their health history, and previous family and social situation, including their experiences in the care system.

It is good practice for the medical adviser to meet with prospective adopters to share all appropriate health information and to discuss the needs of the child with whom you are matched. It is also good practice to provide a written report of this meeting.

THE ADOPTION REGISTER FOR ENGLAND AND WALES

The Adoption Register has two major elements:

- A computer database that stores details of children awaiting adoption where their own agency has not been able to find the right adoptive family, and details of approved adopters awaiting a placement where their own agency has not been able to match them with appropriate children; and

- A staff team of experienced database operators and family placement social workers who will look at the information to see whether they can suggest possible "matches" between children and prospective adopters.

Agencies refer to the Register those children who have been authorised to be placed for adoption but where there is not already a link identified locally which is being actively pursued. The children will be referred at the latest by three months after the agency has formally decided that a child should be placed for adoption and either:

- a placement order has been granted; or

- an application has been made for a placement order and all required consents, including that of the court, have been obtained; or

- the consent to placement for adoption has been obtained from parents with parental responsibility.

Children

If you are a prospective adopter, you will be able to contact the Register direct on the helpline (see below). Once your identity has been checked, the Register will confirm that your details have been referred to them, give you information about the number of times your details have been sent out to social workers for consideration, and give you general advice. If your details have been sent out for consideration but a link is not being pursued, you can contact your social worker and ask about the reasons given by the child's social worker for not pursuing the link.

Families

Agencies can refer prospective adopters to the Adoption Register as soon as they have been approved by the agency and will usually do this if it seems unlikely that the adopters will be matched quickly with a suitable child in their own region. Agencies must refer prospective adopters (with their consent) to the Adoption Register three months after they have been approved if there is not a match with an identified child being actively pursued. You can decide that you do not wish to give your consent to referral to the Adoption Register but this will, of course, reduce the opportunity for you to be matched with an appropriate child.

If your agency has not already sent your details to the Adoption Register, you will be able to refer yourself to the Register. You must wait to do this until at least three months after the date on which your agency approved you as an adopter.

Matching children with adoptive families

Once your details have been recorded on the Register database, a search will be undertaken to identify child(ren) who match your approval profile. Relevant details of your family, including a written description (profile) and details of your approving agency will be sent to the child(ren)'s social worker who will consider the proposed link further. Information about your family can initially be sent out up to five times to different social workers for consideration. At this point your register entry will be put "on hold" whilst the social workers are given time to pursue possible links with any of the children.

Adoption Register for England and Wales
Unit 4, Pavilion Business Park
Royds Hall Road, Wortley
Leeds LS12 6AJ
Adopter's helpline: 0870 750 2176
Email: mail@adoptionregister.org.uk
www.adoptionregister.org.uk

Scotland's Adoption Register

Funded by the Scottish Government and launched in 2011, Scotland's Adoption Register is run by BAAF Scotland and has two major functions:

- to provide facts and figures about adoption in Scotland;

- to add an effective Scotland-wide mechanism to existing arrangements for linking children and families for adoption.

Scotland's Adoption Register
113 Rose Street
Edinburgh EH2 3DT
Tel: 0131 226 9279
Email: sar@scotlandsadoptionregister.org.uk
www.scotlandsadoptionregister.org.uk

ARIS – Adoption Regional Information System Northern Ireland

Operated by BAAF on behalf of the Department of Health, Social Services and Public Safety (DHSSPS), ARIS operates on a similar basis to the Adoption Register.
ARIS NI
Botanic House
1–5 Botanic Avenue
Belfast BT7 1JG
Tel: 028 9031 9070
email: aris@baaf.org.uk
www.ni-aris.org.uk

Considering ethnic origin, religion, culture and language when matching a child to a family

In general, it is in a child's best interest to be placed with parents who share as many aspects of their culture, ethnic background, language and religion as possible. Several studies have shown that these aspects of a child's background play an important role in developing a strong identity and in influencing the child's social adjustment as an adult. The welfare checklist in section 1 of the Adoption and Children Act 2001 requires agencies to take into account, when making decisions about adoption, the child's religious persuasion, racial origin and cultural and linguistic background.

Social workers, therefore, must give due consideration to these aspects when matching a child to a prospective family, but they must also consider the adoptive families which are available and the ability of those families to meet most of the child's needs. Guidance 3.16 states that 'while children do tend to do better if adopted by a family who shares their ethnic origin or cultural group, these are just one of many considerations and must not be the primary consideration...' 'The core issue is what qualities, experiences and attributes the prospective adopter can draw on and their level of understanding of the discrimination and racism the child may be confronted with when growing up' (Guidance 4.7).

HELPFUL BOOKS

In Search of Belonging: Reflections by transracially adopted people,
Edited by Perlita Harris, BAAF, 2006
The first UK publication to give voice to transracially adopted children and adults. Brings together poetry, artwork, memoir, writing and oral testimony from over 50 transracial and transnational UK adoptees.

To find out as much as you can about the prospective child:

- Talk to adults who know the child well.

- Discuss the Child's Permanence Report fully with social workers.

- Ask for a Child/Life Appreciation Day. This is a day when significant people in the child's life are invited to meet with the adopters to share information about the child. These people could include former foster carers, teachers, health visitors, child minders and former social workers. Family members may be involved too. Those involved will be able to share anecdotes and stories which may not be included in more formal reports.

- Meet significant family members and friends. The agency should have prepared you for the advantages of meeting the birth parent/s even if direct contact may not continue. Many adopters see this as important for the child's future.

- Have access to relevant sections of the child's file.

- Talk to foster carers about ways in which they handle any difficulties.

- Consider the proposals for contact and whether you are comfortable with them.

- Receive and discuss a proposed written Adoption Support Plan.

When considering placement of a child with a family from a different cultural background or ethnicity, social workers will want to be certain that the prospective adopters recognise that their own experiences may inhibit their complete understanding of, for example, racism that the child may encounter in the future. Social workers will also assess the prospective adopters' ability to help the child value, understand and experience various aspects of his or her own ethnicity and culture of origin, and to promote cultural continuity for that child.

Guidance 4.8 recognises that adopters will need flexible and creative support to be given by their agency. This could involve training sessions and providing opportunities for children to meet others from similar backgrounds and to practise their religion of origin.

A question of "competition"...?

Many prospective adopters are, understandably, irritated when they discover that several families may be considered, simultaneously, for one child. Adopters may feel upset that they have been placed "in competition" with other adopters in such a delicate matter. And, practically speaking, it seems a waste of resources – after all, aren't there hundreds of children waiting to be adopted?

However, it is important to remember that the child's welfare must always be the paramount consideration and that the key tasks are to find the adoptive family best able to meet the child's needs and to find them as quickly as possible. For these reasons, it may be necessary for several families to be considered at the same time before a decision is made about which one to concentrate on.

When considering more than one prospective adopter, social workers will consider issues of ethnicity, culture, religion, and language; the child's attachment issues, behavioural issues, personality, health, disabilities (if any), education, status in family (e.g. eldest/only), and physical characteristics (appearance); the child's wishes and birth parents' wishes; interests/hobbies/talents of child and adopters; contact requirements; and adopters' geographic location.

Although the child's agency may approach several adoptive families about a child, they must only present one adoptive family to the panel for a match with a child.

Do siblings have to be placed together?

In many cases, yes; in some, no. Children who are generally placed together include those who have a strong bond with each other and will benefit from staying together as a group.

In other cases, children may need particularly focused attention from the adopter/s, or may have other physical or emotional needs that are best met if the child is placed as an "only child". If a child suffers from extreme difficulties with attachment, placement as an only child may also be less stressful for the adoptive parent.

Sometimes large groups are split into twos and threes to allow families to more easily come forward to parent them. If a child is placed away from his or her siblings, it will be very important to consider arrangements for the children to have some contact with each other, if this meets the child's needs.

For more information about this topic, see:

- **Together or Apart? Assessing brothers and sisters for permanent placement** by Jenifer Lord and Sarah Borthwick, BAAF, 2008
  A practice guide which highlights factors affecting decisions on placements of sibling groups.

- **We Are Family: Sibling relationships in placement and beyond** by Audrey Mullender (ed.), BAAF, 1999
  An anthology that explores sibling placements from diverse perspectives.

HELPFUL BOOKS

Life Story Work: What it is and what it means by Shaila Shah and Hedi Argent, BAAF, 2006.
This is a guide for children that explains what life story work is, why it is important to do it, and how you can do it.

My Life and Me by Jean Camis, BAAF, 2001.
This is a book that you can use with the child as part of the life story work which may need to be undertaken.

Life Story Work by Tony Ryan and Rodger Walker, BAAF, 1999.
This excellent guide provides insight, creative ideas and exercises you could use to do life story work in different settings.

- **Siblings in Late Permanent Placements** by Alan Rushton *et al,* BAAF, 2001
  A research study that explores the complexities of sibling placements and evaluates the outcomes in a sample of 1,330 children.

- **The Placement of Large Sibling Groups in Adoption** by Hilary Saunders and Julie Selwyn, BAAF, 2011
  A research study that considers what motivates adopters to take a large sibling group, examines the support available, the different agency practices, and the challenges and rewards.

6 The adoption panel considers the proposed match and makes a recommendation

You and the child should not be formally matched until the child has been authorised to be placed for adoption by the granting of a placement order or formal parental consent has been given.

Your social worker and the child's social worker and managers will meet to decide whether to support the match as being the right one for the child and for you. If they decide that it is, the social worker then completes an adoption placement report if you as prospective adopters agree that you want to go ahead. This report must be given to you at least ten days before the adoption panel considers the proposed match. You can comment on any of the content of the report. Adoption regulations set out what is required in this report.

Within the adoption placement report, the social worker must include:

- the agency's reasons for proposing the placement;

- your views about the proposed placement;

- your views about the proposed contact arrangements;

- the agency's proposals for adoption support services for the adoptive family;

- the agency's proposals for contact.

At this stage, the adoption panel will be familiar with the child's records and with his or her specific needs. It will be the panel of the child's agency that will consider the match, which may or may not be the one which considered your approval. It will operate in a similar way and you will be invited to attend.

Legally, the adoption panel is required to undertake the considerations and recommendations with the child's welfare as the paramount consideration. Panel members will be aware that they must carefully balance the disadvantages of children remaining looked after by their local authority if the match is not approved, with the burden of ensuring that the applicants really can meet the needs of the child.

The panel will give its recommendation to approve or not approve the match to the agency, which will make the decision. It is unusual that matches are not agreed at this stage, although it can happen. There is no formal appeal process if a match is turned down.

7 You and the child are introduced

The child has been authorised to be placed for adoption. The match with the proposed child has been approved by the adoption panel and the agency – and by you. *Before* you meet the child, your social worker should give you the Adoption Placement Plan, setting out:

- the agency's reasons for proposing the placement;

- your views on the proposed placement and the agency's proposed contact arrangements;

- the local authority's proposal for adoption support services for the adoptive family;

- the agency's proposals for allowing contact by any person; and

- any other relevant information.

You should also take this opportunity to express any concerns or ask questions you may have. You and the agency will then agree a detailed introduction plan.

If the child is a baby, he or she may be placed with you fairly quickly. If the child is older, you will have a series of meetings with him or her before the child is placed. The purpose of these **introductions** is not only to meet the child, but also to help you and the child find out what living together will be like. You can do this by going through daily activities and routines,

One of the keys to successful introductions is... the capacity of the adults concerned to work together in the interests of the child...This means acknowledging that adopters bring skills and knowledge to the placement process. Their experience of the child may be different from that of previous carers, as permanence brings with it a far more loaded emotional agenda. Listening to, reviewing with and empowering prospective adoptive parents will generally facilitate positive outcomes.

S. Byrne, *Linking and Introductions*, BAAF, 2000, p.10

meeting friends and neighbours, looking at common interests, and focusing on the particular needs of the child.

A child cannot be placed with you until you have notified the child's agency that you wish the placement to happen.

What happens during the introductions?

During the introductions, you will first meet the child at his or her foster home. You will spend a few hours with the child, initially, and gradually spend more time on successive days. You can take this time to observe the child's interactions with the foster carer and to discuss the child's general behaviour and habits (eating, dressing, playing, likes/dislikes, etc).

After visiting the child in the foster home, the child will spend time at your house during the day and, eventually, may stay overnight and return to the foster home the next day. The length of time the introductory period takes depends entirely upon you and the child – older children may take longer to adjust to you (and you to them). You may also feel pressured by school term dates, holidays or other activities. But "speeding up" the process to meet these dates may not be in your or the child's best interests.

You can help the child adjust to the idea of moving in with you. Once you have been matched with the child, you will be asked to create a book for the child that tells about yourself and your family, and what it is like to live at your house. You can include photos of yourself, your home, family, neighbours, pets, and daily or favourite activities. It is helpful, especially for young children, to enable the child to "interact" with the book (by providing crayons or stickers with the book), thus making it his or her own (see *Helpful books* below).

Oh, the stress of it!

Spending time with the child at the foster carer's home can be a stressful experience for prospective adopters. You undoubtedly will be anxious to establish your own relationship with the child and you may find it difficult if the child is fairly attached to the foster carer. In addition, you may not agree with various ways in which the foster carer interacts with the child.

HELPFUL BOOKS

Me and my Family by Jean Maye, BAAF, 2011
A unique, interactive and fun "welcome to our family" book through which adopters can initially introduce themselves to the child, and for the child to work through and record the changes in their lives as they move to their new family. With space for drawings, writing and photographs.

It is important to remember, however, that these first visits are meant for you to observe the child so you can determine how best to meet his or her needs. Candid discussions with the foster carer(s) can give you valuable insight into the child that will help everyone in the long run.

8 The child moves in (i.e. is placed with you)

In preparation for the child moving to your home, you will have a **final planning meeting** with your social worker, the child's social worker, foster carer/s, teachers – and anyone else significantly involved with the child – to discuss the placement date and to confirm details of the Adoption Placement Plan.

The Adoption Placement Plan

When an agency has decided on a placement it must provide 'as soon as possible' a *written adoption placement plan* to the prospective adopters.

Content of Adoption Placement Plan – Schedule 5, Adoption Agency Regulations 2005

1   Whether the child is to be placed under a **placement order** or **consent of the parent/guardian**.

2   The arrangements for **preparing the child** and the prospective adopters for the placement.

3   The **date on which it is proposed to place the child** with the prospective adopters.

4   The arrangements for **review** of the placement.

5   **Whether the parental responsibility for the prospective adopters is to be restricted** and if so, the extent to which it is to be restricted.

6   **The support services** to be provided for the adoptive family.

7   **The agency's arrangements for allowing any person contact** with the child, the form of contact, the arrangements for supporting contact and the name and details of the person responsible for facilitating the contact arrangements (if applicable).

8   **The dates on which the child's life story book and later-life letter are to be provided** by the adoption agency to the prospective adopters.

9   Details of **any other arrangements** that need to be made.

10   **Contact details** for the child's social worker, the prospective adopters' social worker and out-of-hours contacts.

This final planning meeting will help everyone involved to understand each others' roles, responsibilities and expectations during the post-placement period. For example, you will want to know:

- the extent to which both social workers will be involved with the child during the placement;

- what contact (if any) the child will have with the birth family;

- if the child will have any continued contact with foster carers;

- what arrangements need to be made with other services (health, education) and who should arrange them; and

- what adoption support services are to be provided and when and how they are to be provided.

Contact

Research has shown that in many cases, adopted children can benefit from some form of contact with their birth parent and/or relatives. This can help a child have a sense of their history and heritage.

Contact after adoption may be planned if it is believed to be in the child's best interests. This may occur via "letterbox" or "indirect" contact, in which the adoptive parents agree to provide written information about the child and perhaps a photo, once every year. The letter is sent to the agency, from where it is then forwarded to the birth parent. The birth parent can provide information to the child in the same way.

Contact may also occur directly, between the birth parent/s – and/or other members of the birth family – and child, by visits or meetings in public places (local restaurant, park, etc). It is important to remember that contact issues should always be decided with the child's interests in mind.

Where children have been authorised to be placed for adoption, or placed for adoption by an agency (including those under six weeks of age), contact is at the discretion of the local authority – there is not a duty to promote contact.

The child, the local authority, parents, guardians, relatives, holders of a previous contact or residence order, and those who had care of the child by a High Court order, can apply under section 26 of the Adoption and Children Act 2002 for a contact order. When the court makes a placement order it must consider actual or proposed contact arrangements, and the views of the parties, and may make a contact order even if there has been no application for one. Others, including the child's prospective adopters, can apply for section 26 contact orders with leave of the court.

Contact after adoption: It is not uncommon for an arrangement to be made for some form of continuing contact (often indirect, for example, by means of letters or cards) to continue after adoption between the child and members of his or her birth family.

Before making an adoption order the court has a duty to consider whether there should be arrangements for contact (orders or undertakings) and hear the views of all the parties. There is no "presumption" of contact.

TERMS YOU MAY NEED TO KNOW...

Children's Guardian: a person appointed by the court to protect the child's interests during court proceedings for care orders and placement orders. This person might talk with the child to ensure there are no remaining issues that may affect the proposed match with the family. Because the child should not be matched with you until the placement order has been granted, the guardian will not need to visit you during care or placement order proceedings.

Curator *at litem* (in Scotland): has a role similar to that of the Children's Guardian.

Disruption: a term used to describe adoptions that do not work out. When a placement "disrupts", the child is returned to the care of the agency that originally placed him or her with you. A disruption meeting should be convened, followed by counselling or other support for the adoptive family (see also Section 5 of this Handbook).

Later-life letter: A letter written to the child, by a social worker, that explains (in children's terms) why the child was placed for adoption and how the placement occurred. The Adoption Placement Report should say when the later-life letter (and the child's life story book) will be provided.

Life story book: A "book" prepared with the child by a social worker, foster carer and/or adoptive parent that documents the child's life, from birth, through his or her life in foster care or residential care, to adoption. The information may include a description of the child's birth parent/s and/or birth family, other siblings or half-siblings, where that child was born, foster carers, and how the child came to be adopted. The purpose of the book is to provide a link for the child (when he or she is old enough to understand it) with his or her past and life history. The book is given to the adoptive parents who use the information sensitively, with the understanding that it belongs to the child. Where no such book exists, you can work on completing one with the child.

Reporting Officer: a social worker independent of the adoption agency who is appointed by the court to witness the birth parents' consent to their child's placement for adoption (section 19).

Section 8 contact orders can be made with adoption orders on application by parents and guardians, or others with leave of the court, or on the court's own initiative.

Birth family members or others seeking a section 8 contact order under the Adoption and Children Act 2002 after an adoption order has been granted, must first obtain leave of the court to apply.

HELPFUL RESOURCES

Guidelines for a Letterbox for Adopted Children (1988)
Maintaining Links with Birth Families: a leaflet for adoptive parents (1995)
Both leaflets are available from Adoption UK (see Appendix 2). See Section 4 for more information about resources for adopted people who are seeking contact with birth relatives.

Contact in Adoption and Permanent Foster Care: Research, theory and practice edited by Elsbeth Neil and David Howe, BAAF, 2004.

Staying Connected: Managing contact arrangements in adoption edited by Hedi Argent, BAAF, 2002.

Contact in Adoption a video which features adoptive parents talking about their experiences with contact. Available from Faith in Families, Nottingham (see Appendix 2).

What is Contact? A guide for children by Hedi Argent, BAAF, 2004.

Adoptive parents are *not* required to agree to contact, but may be advised to do so if social workers believe it will benefit the child. It is also important to remember that, as children grow up, they may seek to have contact with birth parents and relatives, and may search for them.

When is the best time for the child to move?

There really is no "best" or "worst" time for placement. Generally, you will want to arrange moving in to suit the child. For school-age children, this means thinking about whether the child will need to change schools and when will be the best time to do this. Moving in during school holidays may not be ideal, because there will be less structure and routine in the child's life, which he or she may find unsettling. You and the child will also have constant interaction during holiday periods, which may prove difficult for both of you at the start of a placement.

The child generally benefits if your life continues "as normal" after moving in. "Celebrating" the event with large parties or exotic holidays will disrupt the child's normal routine and will make it harder for the child to adjust to the new family and surroundings. After all, returning from holiday or settling down after a party will entail another "change" for a child who has just experienced one of the most stressful changes in his or her young life.

You will need to arrange:

- an appointment with your GP and/or practice nurse to introduce the child and to discuss any questions you might have about the child's health records;

- visits with schools or playgroups (if the child will have to change to a new one).

  Your local authority must inform your GP and the education department of the child's placement with you. If the child is three years old or younger, your local health visitor should arrange to visit you. If this does not happen, contact your GP's surgery to make the appointment.

  You may also wish to consult the GP with whom your child was registered while he or she was in foster care.

  You should receive your child's health record book from your social worker. This lists your child's NHS number, immunisations, a growth record and other significant health information. If this record book is not available, ask your GP to provide a new one for your child. You will also have health information about the child in the Child's Permanence Report.

Having a child move in will almost be like giving birth. Do I have any legal basis for taking time off work?

Yes. Statutory adoption leave and statutory adoption pay (SAP) and also statutory paternity leave and statutory paternity pay (SPP) are now available.

SAP and adoption leave are available to employees (male or female) adopting a child. They could be adopting on their own, or with their spouse or civil partner.

- SAP is paid for a maximum of 39 weeks at the lower of £124.88 (currently) or 90% of average weekly earnings.

- Adoption leave is available for 52 weeks but only the first 39 weeks are covered by SAP.

- To qualify for adoption leave the adopter must have completed 26 weeks' continuous service with their employer by the end of the week in which they are notified of being matched with a child.

  An adopter who wishes to receive SAP and take adoption leave will need to give their employer documentary evidence to confirm that they are adopting a child through an adoption agency. You will need a Matching Certificate, issued by your adoption agency, once you have been formally matched with a child.

Statutory paternity pay (SPP) and paternity leave are available to employees (male or female) who are the partner of someone adopting a child on their own or adopting a child with their spouse or civil partner.

- SPP and paternity leave can be taken for one or two whole weeks.

- SPP is paid at the lower of £124.88 (currently) or 90% of average weekly earnings.

- To qualify for paternity leave the employee must have completed 26 weeks continuous service with their employer by the end of the week in which the adopter is notified of having been matched with a child.

An adopter (or their partner) who wishes to take SPP and paternity leave will need to give their employer evidence of their entitlement and will need information from the adoption agency for this. This is the Matching Certificate, described above.

If a couple is adopting a child jointly, the couple must choose who takes the SAP and adoption leave and who takes the SPP and paternity leave.

SAP and adoption leave and SPP and paternity leave are not normally available to foster carers adopting without the approval of the child's local authority or to step-parents who adopt a child – this is because these are not *agency* adoptions.

Employees who adopt a child from overseas (or whose partner does) may be eligible for SAP and adoption leave and SPP and paternity leave – the entitlements are the same as for those adopting a child in the UK. However, because of the differences in procedure for adoptions from overseas, the eligibility and evidential requirements are different:

- To qualify for either adoption or paternity leave employees must have 26 weeks' continuous service with their employer: that is, either 26 weeks ending with the week in which the adopter receives official notification or 26 weeks from the start of their employment.

- The information and evidence which employees must provide for paternity leave/SPP and adoption leave/SAP is written notification issued by the central authority that the adopter is eligible to adopt and has been assessed or approved as a suitable adoptive parent.

Both paternity and adoption leave can only start once the child has entered Great Britain.

It is important to keep your employer informed. You must notify your employer of your intention to take adoption leave or paternity leave within seven days of the date the adoption agency tells you that you have been matched with a child.

More information is available from:

- www.adoptionuk.org.uk

- Guidance is also available at www.direct.gov.uk

- ACAS on 08457 474747 www.acas.org.uk

- Current figures for pay are available on the Department for Work and Pensions website at www.direct.gov.uk

If you are ineligible for SAP because of low earnings, short length of service or self-employment, you could ask the child's local authority to consider making a payment of financial support equivalent to SAP under the Adoption Support Services Regulations 2005. A move was launched in the Commons in early 2011 to give adoptive parents the same benefits as birth parents in relation to leave, pay and allowances. This, if successful, would enable those on low earnings or benefits and self-employed adopters to receive adoption pay.

9. An adoption order is made through the court

HELPFUL GUIDE

Adoption: A guide for court users (Form A20), available at www.adoption.org.uk or www.hmcourts-service.gov.uk

The child's "legal" position

The child will not be your child, legally, until an adoption order is made by a court (see Section 2). You will have a "settling in" time, during which the social workers will visit you and the child at your home. You can apply for an adoption order at any time after the child has lived with you for ten weeks (if the child was placed with you by an agency). However, in agency placements you will share parental responsibility for the child from the time of placement.

The adoption certificate

Once the adoption is legalised by the courts, the child's adoption certificate is issued. This lists the adoptive family's surname and the date of the adoption order and the court where it was made. The child's actual birth certificate remains unchanged and can be accessed when the child is 18, or earlier if the child's birth name and the name of the birth mother are known. There is a short version of the adoption certificate which only lists the child's adoptive name and does not mention adoption. The certificate is available from the General Register Office for England and Wales or from the General Register Office for Scotland, or the Registrar General in Northern Ireland (See Appendix 2).

Can the birth parents oppose the making of the adoption order when the papers reach the court, even if the child has been placed with you for some time?

This is a complex question that depends upon the legal status of the child. If the parents have consented to the child's placement for adoption or have not withdrawn their consent, or the court has granted a placement

HELPFUL BOOKS

Adopted Children Speaking by Caroline Thomas and Verna Beckford, BAAF, 1999
This book offers moving and poignant testimonies and valuable insights into what children feel about adoption, including waiting for a family, moving in, and the involvement of the courts.

Adopters on Adoption: Reflections on parenthood and children by David Howe, BAAF, 1996
An absorbing collection of personal stories that covers assessment and preparation, feelings towards birth family members, parenting issues and the experience of adopting.

The Colours in Me: Writing and poetry by adopted children and young people, edited by Perlita Harris, BAAF, 2008
A unique collection of poetry, prose and artwork by over 80 young contributors – ranging from 4–20 years of age – who reveal what it feels like and what it means to be adopted. Also available, a DVD containing readings from *The Colours in Me*.

Could You be my Parent? Adoption and fostering stories edited by Leonie Sturge-Moore, BAAF, 2005
A collection of articles and interviews taken from BAAF's family-finding newspaper, *Be My Parent*, which create a fascinating snapshot of the process of adoption and foster care.

The Dynamics of Adoption: Social and personal perspectives, edited by Amal Treacher and Ilan Katz, Jessica Kingsley Publishers, 2000
A collection of essays about numerous aspects of adoption. This book is not a practical guide to adoption, rather a collection of thoughts about aspects of adoption.

Intercountry Adoption: Developments, trends and perspectives, edited by Peter Selman, BAAF, 2000
An anthology that explores several aspects of intercountry adoption from a variety of perspectives including those of "sending" countries, "receiving" countries, adopters, adopted people and researchers.

order for the child, then the birth parents cannot oppose the making of the adoption order unless the court gives them permission to do so. For more information about this and about the court process, see Section 2 of this guide.

Can we travel outside of the UK for a holiday with our child, if he or she has been placed with us, but the adoption has not yet been legalised in the courts?

Yes. If the adoption order has not yet been made, you must inform children's services of your intention to travel abroad. They will provide a letter giving you permission to take the child abroad. You must carry this letter with you, to avoid any difficulties with immigration officers who may question why you have a different surname from that of your child. If your child does not have a passport, you must have one issued in his or her birth name. You cannot take the child out of the UK for more than one month without the permission of the court or the permission of the birth parents with parental responsibilities.

10 Settling in and post-placement support

'... there is no single factor that leads to success or to instability in a placement, but the way in which several factors combine and interact.'

R. Parker, *Adoption Now: Messages from Research*, Department of Health, 1999, p.15

As your child settles in to live with you and your family, you will continue to receive support from your social worker and from the child's social worker.

Statutory visits

The child's social worker (and possibly your social worker) will visit the child at your home within the first week. After that, they must visit at least once a week until the first review at four weeks to see how the child and you are settling in together. The social worker will arrange a statutory review within four weeks of the placement. Another review will follow three months after the first, and then six-monthly until the adoption order is granted. It is important to view these visits as a useful means of gathering support and information, rather than an intrusive invasion of your privacy. You and the child will gain the most benefit from these visits if you are candid with the social worker and raise the questions or issues that concern you.

What should I do if the child behaves badly during the social worker's visit?

Don't be afraid to treat your child "normally" – as you would if the social worker was not present. Most social workers have had many years' experience with children and will be well aware that the child may be very attention seeking or may behave badly during these visits. It will help your child if your response to him or her is consistent, no matter what the circumstances.

What do older children feel when being placed with a new family?

It is always helpful to try to put yourself in the child's shoes. How would you have felt, for example, at the age of four, upon moving in with a family of people you had met only a few weeks ago? The child may feel anxious, worried, perhaps somewhat frightened. He or she will need to understand the moving-in process in his or her "own" way. Social workers can help you and the child by giving the child as much information as possible in an "age-appropriate" way, explaining the purpose of the "introductions", and by providing information about you. Many foster carers also prepare the child for this event from the moment he or she arrives in their home.

You can also talk with your social worker about how best to minimise the child's anxiety, for example, by continuing contact with the foster family, the child's friends and activities, etc.

TERMS YOU MAY NEED TO KNOW...

Intermediary services – a service provided by some adoption agencies on behalf of birth relatives. The agency sends a letter to the adoptive parents or adopted adults, informing them of the interest of a birth relative. Birth relatives are not provided with identifying information unless the adopted person agrees. This service is now offered by all adoption agencies following implementation of the Adoption and Children Act 2002.

Adoption Contact Register for England and Wales – a database of names and contact information of adopted people over 18 and their birth relatives. Either party can contact the Register. The Register enables both parties to declare an interest before either can act. In Scotland, this service is provided by **Birthlink.** (See Appendix 2.)

Support after the adoption

Parenting an adopted child is not always a straightforward matter. There may be problems that crop up many months or years after the child is placed with you (see Section 4). You may have brief questions, from time to time, or you may need specific services and ongoing support to help you with the child.

Settling-in grants

These are available for most children if they are needed. For details about these grants and about other financial support, see Section 2.

Whatever your needs, the adoption support provided by your local authority, adoption agency and other specialist post-adoption organisations can help you address issues you may face along the way. See Section 5 and Appendix 2 for more information about adoption support.

In addition to support from your local authority, the following organisations provide post-adoption support.

- Adoption UK (www.adoptionuk.org.uk)

- Post-adoption centres in different parts of the country

- Some voluntary adoption agencies

See Section 5 for contact details.

Adoption support services

Adoption Support Services Regulations 2005 and accompanying Guidance came into force on 30 December 2005. (There are equivalent regulations for Wales.) These place a duty on local authorities to assess the support needs of children and adopters with whom they are making placements and to decide what services will be offered, before the placement goes ahead.

Local authorities must appoint an Adoption Support Services Adviser (ASSA) who has responsibility for ensuring that people are directed towards appropriate services and that these are available. This will include a liaison role with health and education authorities and with local authorities and voluntary adoption agencies. Local authorities are required to publicise the identity and contact details of their ASSA.

Social networking and contact

Social networking sites such as Facebook have had a huge impact on the way that people communicate with each other. Finding and contacting people is much easier than ever before, with both positive and negative outcomes.

it is important that you are aware of the way that the use of the internet, social network and other technologies such as i-phones are changing the whole context of adoption contact. You need to know what you can do to protect privacy and security in the best interests of your child. However, you also need to recognise that there is a limit to how far you can control and monitor the use of these new forms of contact by your child and/ or members of their birth family. You may need to manage complex situations which arise from unauthorised and unmediated contact.

HELPFUL BOOKS

Facing up to Facebook: A survival guide for adoptive families Eileen Fursland, BAAF, 2010
Examines the way the internet, social networking and other technologies are changing the landscape of adoption contact, search and reunion. Provides essential information and advice.

Social Networking and You Eileen Fursland, BAAF, 2011
A booklet for adopted young people on using social networking. Offers practical advice on sharing information (or not) and staying safe online.

HELPFUL GUIDES

Intercountry Adoption An introductory guide which details legislation, procedures and processes, BAAF, 2006

A Guide to Intercountry Adoption for UK residents published by the Department of Health, May 2003. Available at www.education.gov.uk/ publications

Intercountry Adoption Procedural Guide, available from the Intercountry Adoption Centre. www.icacentre.org.uk

Intercountry adoptions

Adopters may wish to adopt babies or toddlers from overseas, as there are few babies needing adopting in the UK, or they may have been moved by the plight of children abandoned in orphanages or affected by war or disasters in the countries they were born in.

The Adoption and Children Act 2002 and the Adoptions with a Foreign Element Regulations 2005 provide for the regulation of intercountry adoption in England and Wales.

• Anyone wishing to adopt from overseas, including relatives, must be approved as adopters for intercountry adoption by a local authority or by a voluntary adoption agency registered to do this work.

• It is a criminal offence to bring a child who is not "habitually resident" in the UK to the UK for adoption without complying with these regulations.

How do I apply to adopt from abroad?

You can obtain preliminary information about intercountry adoption from the overseas Adoption Helpline, BAAF, or the Department for Education (DfE) Adoption Website (see Appendix 2 for contact details). The general process is then:

1 Contact your local authority children's services/social work department. It has a duty to provide, or to arrange to provide, a service for people wishing to be approved as intercountry adopters. It will supply general information and counselling about adoption. It will also discuss with you the children waiting for adoption in the UK. Some applicants may then choose to adopt in the UK; others will continue with intercountry adoption.

2 You must check the specific requirements of the overseas country of your choice. Some countries will not accept gay, lesbian or single adopters and some have rules about the maximum and minimum ages of prospective

adopters. The DfE lists some countries as "designated" and others as "non-designated" for adoption. If you adopt from a "non-designated" country, you will have to "re-adopt" the child after you bring him or her to the UK. Your local authority will be involved in supervising the child's placement and will prepare a report for the UK court that will consider the adoption application. If you adopt from a "designated" country, you will have an adoption hearing in that country and will not have to re-adopt the child once you return to the UK. There are also countries which, like the UK, have ratified the Hague Convention on intercountry adoption. You will not need to re-adopt here if you adopt under the Hague Convention. (These countries are listed on www.education.gov.uk.)

3   Your local authority will arrange for a home study to be done or you can apply to one of the eight voluntary adoption agencies which are approved to assess the suitability of intercountry adoption and applicants. They all cover specific and limited geographical catchment areas. Applicants usually have to pay for this service. Charges vary among agencies but are currently often £6,000 or more. The home study will cover the same issues as for domestic adoption (see p. 19). The social worker will record details of the home study on the Prospective Adopters' Report. The Department of Education charges applicants in England and Wales a fee for its part of the process (see points 7, 8 and 10 below). This is currently £1,775. However, there is a means test and applicants wishing to adopt a close relative from overseas will be exempt. The overall cost of intercountry adoption is likely to be at least £20,000.

4   An adoption panel will consider your application and make a recommendation.

5   The agency decides whether or not to approve your application.

6   If your application is approved, it is sent, along with the Prospective Adopter's Report and the medical form, adoption panel minutes and other paperwork to the DfE or the Welsh Assembly Government (the Central Authority).

7   The Central Authority will decide whether or not to issue a **Certificate of Approval**.

8   If you are approved, the Central Authority will send your papers to the authorities of the country from which you wish to adopt.

9   The agency in the child's country considers your application.

10 If the agency approves your application, your name is placed on a waiting list. When a child is identified, information about the child is sent to the Central Authority, which then sends it on to you. You should discuss this information with your agency's social worker, its medical adviser and/or your GP.

11 You travel to the child's country to meet the child. If you are married or civil registered, both of you must go to meet the child.

12 You must apply for UK immigration entry clearance for the child, and must fulfil the requirements of the child's country of origin (for example, completing paperwork and providing fees, if any).

Will my adopted child automatically become a British citizen?

A child adopted outside the UK does not automatically receive British citizenship, even if both adoptive parents are British. The parents must apply for British citizenship for that child. A child adopted in the UK will become a British citizen if one of the adoptive parents is a British citizen. The exception to this is a child who is adopted by British citizens under Hague Convention procedures. He or she will receive British citizenship from the date of the adoption.

Health issues for children adopted from overseas

There may be very little medical information about a child adopted from overseas. It is important to be aware that the child may have an inherited condition that might not become obvious until he or she is older. You must also be aware that the child may have been exposed to infectious diseases, such as HIV, hepatitis B, hepatitis C, or tuberculosis, and that testing for these conditions may not be available in the child's own country. There is a high prevalence of pre-natal substance exposure in some countries. You must also be prepared for the possibility that the child has experienced severe abuse and neglect, and may suffer significant effects from this, even if he or she is very young. If the child has been in institutional care, this is likely to have impacted on their opportunity for good early attachments.

it is important that you are aware of these issues and are willing, and able, to address them once you have adopted the child. A BAAF leaflet, *Children Adopted from Abroad: Key health and developmental issues*, is likely to be helpful. The medical adviser should be available to advise prospective adopters on health matters of children being considered for adoption from abroad, and ideally undertake a health assessment of the child.

Will we be entitled to the same adoption support as families who adopt in the UK?

Yes. Children adopted from another country may have a range of special emotional, developmental, health and educational needs, for which you may need specific services and/or post-adoption support (see Sections 4 and 5). However, you should keep in mind that your child's country of origin will usually want evidence that you can financially support the child, before agreeing a match, so you cannot expect to receive financial support to facilitate adoption of a child from overseas.

It will be important to address issues concerning your child's identity and self-esteem. You may find it helpful to seek support from groups and organisations associated with the child's birth country.

HELPFUL ORGANISATIONS

Department for Education: Adoption website

www.dfe.gov.uk/adoption
Offers the latest news relating to the Department's processes for intercountry adoption; about the level of fees charged; and information on recent legislation changes affecting intercountry adoption, both in the UK as well as in particular countries.

Intercountry Adoption Centre

A confidential information and advice service for intercountry adopters at any stage of adoption or post-adoption. Services include an advice line; counselling for families or for young people who were adopted from overseas; training for professionals involved in adoption; and "consultation days" for prospective intercountry adopters.

71–73 High Street, Barnet
Hertfordshire EN5 5UR
Tel: 020 8447 4753
Email: info@icacentre.org.uk
www.icacentre.org.uk

Children and Families Across Borders (CFAB)

A voluntary organisation that helps families and individuals whose lives are split between different countries.

Canterbury Court
1–3 Brixton Road
London SW9 6DE
Tel: 020 7735 8941

Overseas Adoption Support and Information Service (OASIS)

A self-help group that provides information and advice for intercountry adopters, as well as post-adoption support. Produces leaflets and a newsletter, operates an advice line and conducts seminars.

www.adoptionoverseas.org

In addition to the organisations listed here, there are organisations for families who have adopted from particular countries (for example, Children Adopted from China (CACH) and the Adopted Romanian Children's Society (ARC)). Contact the Intercountry Adoption Centre for more information about these groups.

Legal and financial matters

2

In this section:

→ Gain a general understanding of the current laws and regulations concerning adoption and how they may affect you

→ Learn about your legal rights throughout the adoption process and afterwards, and about the rights of the child and the birth parents

→ Find out about the various costs involved with adoption and the financial assistance that may be available to some applicants

Introduction

Adopting a child is a legal process governed by rules and regulations designed to protect everyone involved in the process – most importantly the child, but also the adoptive parents and the birth parents. These laws are designed not only to protect you (and others), but also to help you safeguard your interests. Understanding your legal entitlements and obligations throughout the adoption process, therefore, can help you to be prepared and informed every step of the way.

Before we look at your legal entitlements and obligations throughout the adoption process, it helps to understand the laws that underpin these rights. The main laws in England and Wales are as follows:

- **The Adoption and Children Act 2002** is the statute governing adoption in England and Wales. The welfare of the child is paramount.

- **The Children Act 1989** made the welfare of the child paramount and includes basic principles, such as the definition of parental responsibility, and those followed by the courts in making decisions in children's cases; orders providing for the care and maintenance of children; and the responsibilities of local authorities for children. It is the major statute dealing with child care law and child protection law.

- **The Human Rights Act 1988** gives effect in the UK to rights and freedoms guaranteed under the European Convention on Human Rights.

- **The Protection of Children Act 1999** provides a cross-sector system for identifying people who are considered unsuitable to work with children.

- **The Care Standards Act 2000** governs the inspection and registration of fostering and adoption services. These functions are carried out by Ofsted.

The Adoption and Children Act 2002 was implemented at the end of December 2005. It changed significant parts of the adoption process, particularly in relation to planning for children. It is underpinned by Regulations, Guidance and National Minimum Standards. This chapter looks at legal and financial matters connected with adoption, in light of this new Act. The Act and the regulations are available from The Stationery Office (tel: 0870 600 5522; email: book.orders@tso.co.uk). They can be downloaded at www.education.gov.uk/publications.

There are also many Regulations that govern the way in which adoption agencies carry out their functions (including the function of adoption panels); and those that prohibit agencies from approving adopters or foster carers who have been convicted or have been cautioned for "specified offences". The Adoption Support Services Regulations 2005, and the equivalent in Wales, detail the adoption support duties of local authorities.

HELPFUL BOOKS AND RESOURCES

- **Child Care Law: A summary of the law in England and Wales** by Deborah Cullen and Mary Lane, BAAF, 2006 (5th edition). A popular quick reference guide to the law relating to the care of children.

- **Child Care Law: Scotland** by Alexandra Plumtree, BAAF, 2005 (2nd edition). A popular quick reference guide to the law in Scotland relating to the care of children.

- **Adoption Now: Law, regulations, guidance and standards** by Fergus Smith and Roy Stewart with Alexandra Conroy-Harris, BAAF, 2011 (3rd edition). A handy guide to all adoption legislation in England.

- **Adoption Law for Adopters** by Mary Lane, Adoption UK, 2006

- **Adoption Order application**
  The application form for an Adoption Order can be printed from www.justice.gov.uk or www.hmcourts-service.gov.uk

- **Department for Education: adoption website**
  www.dfe.gov.uk/adoption

For written copies of legislation and explanatory notes about current legislation in the United Kingdom, contact:

- **Office of Public Sector Information (OPSI)**
  To read online and download, visit www.legislation.gov.uk

- **The Stationery Office**
  www.stoshop.co.uk
  Tel: 0870 242 2345 (support line for online orders)
  TSO bookshops are located in Belfast, Birmingham, Cardiff, Edinburgh and London

National Minimum Standards for Adoption

New National Minimum Standards for Adoption were published by the Department for Education in 2011 (see Appendix 3). These standards are designed to improve the quality of adoption practice by informing *everyone* involved in adoption (including children, adopters, birth parents, local authority and voluntary adoption agencies) of what they can expect regarding issues such as timescales for placing children, matching children and families, the decision-making process, and access to services (including adoption support). The standards have the force of formal Guidance.

TERMS YOU MAY NEED TO KNOW

Adoption Order A court order that transfers sole parental responsibility to the adoptive parent/s. An adoption order usually cannot be made unless the child and adopters attend the adoption order hearing at court (unless there are special circumstances preventing the child or one of the adopters from attending). The court can make an order for contact along with the adoption order, although this is very rare.

If the court refuses the adoption order, the court may make another order under the Adoption and Children Act 2002 or the Children Act 1989 – including, for example, a special guardianship order, a residence order, or revising of a placement order.

Care Order A court order giving a local authority parental responsibility for a child which is shared with the child's birth parents, but enables the local authority to make the major decisions about a child's life, such as with whom and where the child should live, and consent to routine medical treatment.

Contact Order When a child is a subject of a placement order or section 19 consent to placement for adoption, there is no duty to provide contact but a contact order can be made under section 26 of the Adoption and Children Act 2002.

A section 8 contact order can be applied for or granted with an adoption order or after an adoption order is granted.

Emergency Protection Order A court order allowing the local authority, in an emergency, either to keep a child in a safe place (such as a hospital or foster home) or to remove a child (e.g. from a home) if it is considered the child is suffering, or is at risk of suffering, significant harm. The local authority must then apply to the court for a care order within the next seven days, if it is believed the child should remain in care to safeguard his or her welfare.

For both an emergency protection order and a care order to be granted by a court, the local authority must satisfy the court that the child is suffering, or is at risk of suffering, significant harm, attributable to an unsatisfactory standard of parental care.

Children's Guardian An officer from CAFCASS (Children and Family Court Advisory and Support Service) appointed by a court when:

i   an application is made by a local authority for a care order or a supervision order for a child; or

ii   when an application is made for a placement order or an adoption order that is opposed by birth parents.

A Children's Guardian may also be appointed in adoption proceedings in other circumstances, such as where there is a dispute about contact arrangements after adoption or the child does not wish to be adopted or is being adopted by relatives. The Children's Guardian is an experienced qualified social worker independent of the local authority.

The Children's Guardian conducts an independent investigation to establish whether or not the care order or placement order applied for is in the interests of the child. He or she meets with the child, the social worker/s and the birth parents. He or she is only likely to meet adopters if parents have been given leave to oppose the making of the adoption order, there is a dispute about contact after the adoption, or the child is being adopted by relatives. The Children's Guardian may also make other relevant investigations, if necessary. He or she then presents the findings to the court, which will then either grant or refuse the order applied for.

Placement Order A court order which gives the local authority the legal entitlement to place a child for adoption. Parental responsibility is shared between the birth parents and the local authority and with the prospective adopters on placement.

Parental Responsibility This is the legal right to make decisions about a child. When a child is born to married parents, both have parental responsibility; if the parents are unmarried, the mother alone has parental responsibility but the father may acquire it by marrying the mother, by formal agreement with the mother or by a court order, or if they jointly register the birth with the mother. Others acquire parental responsibility by adoption – in which case the adoptive parents acquire all the responsibility formerly held by the parents; or by being appointed guardians – in which case they hold the full parental responsibility that a parent has; and in the case of a local authority:

- by the making of a care order, in which case the parent's or guardian's parental responsibility is shared with the local authority;

- or an emergency protection order, which gives the applicant parental responsibility subject to restrictions;

- or a placement order, in which case parental responsibility is shared with the local authority and with the prospective adopters from the time of the placement.

Reporting Officer An officer appointed by a court when a birth parent wishes to consent to the child's placement for adoption, or consent to an adoption order. The Reporting Officer ensures that the parent/s fully understand the legal effect of the consent and have given their consent unconditionally; the Reporting Officer then witnesses the birth parent/s' signed consent. After speaking with the Reporting Officer, if one or both of the birth parents decides not to consent to placement or adoption, the local authority will have to apply for a placement order or the adopters would have to ask the court to dispense with their consent to the making of the adoption order.

Residence Order A court order that determines with whom a child will live, if separated parents cannot agree this. Residence orders are sometimes granted to other relatives such as grandparents, or to foster carers. The making of a residence order discharges a care order. The holder of a residence order shares parental responsibility for the child with the child's parents.

Supervision Order A court order which places the child under the supervision of the local authority. The supervisor's duty is to "advise, assist and befriend" and the court may attach certain requirements to the order. A supervision order does not give the local authority parental responsibility.

Special Guardianship Order A special guardianship order – under section 14 Children Act 1989 – is a "halfway house" between a residence order and an adoption order. The order gives parental responsibility to the special guardians, shared with the birth parents, but allows the special guardians to exercise parental responsibility to the exclusion of the birth parents on most issues (except adoption).

A special guardianship order discharges a care order. The special guardianship order comes to an end when the child is 18 years of age.

Special guardians cannot cause the child to be known under a new surname or be removed from the UK for more than three months without the leave of the court or written permission of each parent with parental responsibility.

Unlike adoption, the legal identity of the child does not change – they remain the child of their birth parents – and their nationality does not change. The birth parents remain liable for child support.

A special guardianship order is intended to be more permanent and legally secure than a residence order but less so than the adoption order, and it will be harder for parents to discharge a special guardianship order than a residence order – they would need permission of the court to apply, and it would only be granted if there had been a significant change in circumstances since the special guardianship order was granted and the welfare of the child required permissions to be given.

Summary of the legal entitlements and legal requirements of people involved in the adoption process

Everyone involved in the adoption process, including birth parents and adoptive parents, has legal entitlements throughout the process, but must also meet the legal requirements of legislation and regulations. These entitlements and requirements are listed in the table below:

THE CHILD

Legal requirements	• A child cannot be adopted once he or she has reached 18 years of age, or is married or civil registered. The application for the adoption order must be made before the child is 18.
	• Before a child can be placed with adoptive parents by an adoption agency, the child's circumstances must be considered, in compliance with regulations, by the agency. The agency must take into account the recommendations of the adoption panel and a decision must be reached about: – whether the child should be placed for adoption – whether a placement order should be applied for.
	• Children placed for adoption within the UK must be placed by an approved adoption agency, unless the placement is with a close relative. A close relative is a grandparent, aunt, uncle or sibling, whether of the full blood or half blood, by marriage or civil partnership.
	• The proposed match between the child and prospective adopters must also be approved by the agency, which will take into account the recommendations of the adoption panel.
	• The child's need for support services after placement and adoption must be assessed and a plan made before matching and placement, and contained within the Adoption Placement Report and Adoption Placement Plan.
Legal entitlements	• The welfare of the child is paramount for the court or agency making decisions about adoption.
	• The child's wishes and feelings about adoption decisions must be given full consideration, taking into account the child's age and ability to understand the issues. In Scotland, children must give written consent to adoption from the age of 12 years.

- All adoptions are registered in the **Adopted Children Register**. At age 18, the person adopted before 30 December 2005 may apply to the Registrar General to obtain a copy of his or her original birth certificate. This is available to adopted persons in Scotland at the age of 16. For people adopted *after* 30 December 2005, the route to disclosure of the original birth certificate and information about their adoption is via an adoption agency, not the Registrar General. If adopted before 12 November 1975, the adopted person must attend an interview with a counsellor before the birth certificate is made available.

- At the age of 18, the adopted person may apply to the Registrar General to be given the name(s) of registered birth relatives listed in the **Adoption Contact Register** wishing to have contact with the adopted person. It must be the adopted person who decides whether or not to contact the relative.

PROSPECTIVE ADOPTERS/ADOPTIVE PARENTS

Legal requirements

- The single adopter or at least one of a couple must be at least 21 years of age and domiciled in the UK or both the adopters must be habitually resident for at least one year in the British Islands.

- A birth parent adopting his child must be at least 18 years old.

- There is no legal upper age limit although adoption agencies need to consider age in relation to the needs of children.

- A person cannot be approved by an agency as an adopter if he/she has a conviction or caution for "specified offences" as described in Section 1 (*Who Can Adopt*) of this guide.

- Single people can adopt, and two people living together as a couple can adopt jointly whether or not they are married or civil registered couples.

- Unless they are a close relative, must be assessed and approved by a UK adoption agency, after taking into account the recommendations of the adoption panel, as well as medical information and other checks regarding suitability (see Section 1 for detailed information).

- Must allow sufficient opportunities for agency social workers and others to visit their home after the child has been placed, to ensure the child's welfare. Those adopting through a local authority agency must also allow the agency to undertake statutory reviews of the placement.

- Those adopting children from overseas must comply with regulations for their approval and for notification of their local authority (see Section 1 for details).

- Prospective agency adopters have parental responsibility for the child placed with them which is shared with the local authority and the birth parents until an adoption order is granted. After the adoption order, only the adopters have parental responsibility.

Legal entitlements

- Prospective adopters are entitled to a fair and prompt service from adoption agencies, in accordance with the **Adoption National Minimum Standards** and **Statutory Adoption Guidance 2011**

- Are entitled to comment and make representations about their assessment by the adoption agency.

- Are entitled to be assessed for support (including financial support) before and after placement and adoption.

- If the child has been made the subject of a care order or placement order for adoption, the birth parent/s of the child cannot remove the child from the adopters without the permission of the local authority holding the order or the leave of a court.

- If the child is placed with prospective adopters and they have filed their application for an adoption order in court, neither the birth parent/s nor the adoption agency can remove the child from the adopters' home without the adopters' permission or the permission of the court, whatever the child's legal status, unless there are child protection concerns.

- Prospective adopters can file their application for an adoption order after the child has lived with them for ten weeks.

- Once the court has granted the adoption order, the adoptive parents have sole parental responsibility for the child. Any previous court orders regarding the child are discharged unless a section 8 contact order is made with the adoption order (very rare).

- If prospective adopters do not wish to continue to care for the child placed with them, they can ask for the child to be returned to the agency, which must receive the child.

BIRTH PARENTS

Legal requirements

- Birth fathers who are not married to the birth mother can acquire parental responsibility by agreement or by court order, by jointly registering the birth with the mother, by marrying the mother or by a parental responsibilities order.

- Only birth parents who have parental responsibility for a child can give consent to the child's placement for adoption or ask the court for permission to oppose the making of the adoption order. If permission to oppose is granted, the court can dispense with the birth parents' consent.

- Consent to the making of an adoption order must be given unconditionally and with full understanding. Evidence of that consent must be available to the court. Consent to placement cannot be given by a birth mother until the child is six weeks old. The birth mother's age is not a factor.

- A birth mother cannot be compelled by law to disclose the identity of the birth father or her own family members.

Legal entitlements

- Birth mothers acquire parental responsibility for their child automatically at the birth, as does a birth father married to the birth mother.

- If a birth mother gives formal consent to her child's placement for adoption, she and a birth father with parental responsibility retain parental responsibility for the child. This entitles her/them to remove the child from the agency's foster care after seven days or from the adoptive placement after 14 days, unless the adopters have applied to the court for an adoption order or unless the agency applies for a placement order.

- Once a child has been authorised to be placed by formal parental consent and/or the granting of a placement order, there is no duty to promote contact but the parents can apply for a Section 26 contact order. Contact is at the discretion of the adoption agency unless a section 26 contact order is made.

- All birth parents must be notified of any decisions made by the agency about their child. This includes:
  - that the child should be placed for adoption;
  - the placement of their child for adoption; and
  - that an adoption order has been applied for.

- Birth parents with parental responsibility are parties to the adoption proceedings and must be notified of the date and court venue of the hearings, and the court can hear their views. Increasingly, birth fathers without parental responsibility will be made parties to adoption and placement proceedings.

LOCAL AUTHORITY/ADOPTION AGENCY
(this information *does not* apply to step-parent or overseas adopters)

Legal requirements	• The agency must ascertain the wishes and feelings of the birth parents about the adoption and about the child's religious and cultural upbringing. The agency must place the child, as far as is practicable, according to these views, as well as taking account of the child's religious persuasion, racial origin and linguistic background.
	• If the whereabouts or identity of the birth father is known, the agency must try, if considered appropriate by the agency, to seek his views about the proposed adoption and offer him a counselling and information service, and ascertain if he intends to acquire parental responsibility for the child.
	• The agency must prepare, and agree with the adopters – before matching panel – an Adoption Placement Report, including contact and support proposals.
	• The agency must inform the local authority in whose area the child is placed, and the health authority, the education department and the adopter's GP when a child is placed.
	• The agency must visit the child in the adoptive home within one week of placement, and each week for the first four weeks. It must review the placement within four weeks of placement, again at three months after placement, and thereafter at six-monthly intervals until an adoption order is granted. The reviews must be chaired by an Independent Reviewing Officer (IRO).
	• When the application for an adoption order is filed with the court, the agency must prepare a court report (known as an Annex A report) concerning the background of the child and birth family, and the adopters, the child's welfare in placement for adoption, the reasons for the agency's decision making, and the agency's opinion as to whether the order applied for is in the child's best interests.
Legal entitlements	• The local authority has parental responsibility for a child who is the subject of formal consent to placement for adoption, and adopters will share parental responsibility with the agency and birth parents from placement.
	• If the local authority holds a placement order or formal consent to placement for the child, it shares parental responsibility with the child's birth parents, but has the power to make major decisions about the child (such as where the child lives and with whom), even if this is against the birth parents' wishes, and make decisions about contact until and unless section 26 contact orders are made.

- The local authority holding a placement order or formal consent to placement is a party to the application for an adoption order and can have its views heard by the court on that application.

The role of the courts in the adoption process

The role of the courts throughout the process of adoption is to ensure that the welfare of the child is paramount and that the legal rights of all parties involved in the process (especially the child's rights) are protected.

Three different courts can undertake adoption proceedings:

- Magistrates Court (known as the Family Proceedings Court)
- County Court Adoption Centre
- High Court

What is the general process for applying for an adoption order?

To apply for an adoption order, you must file an application with the court. If a court has previously made orders involving the child (such as a care order or placement order), then the application for an adoption order should be filed in that same court. The application can subsequently be transferred to another court, e.g. closer to your home area or a County Court Adoption Centre.

You may not require legal advice or representation to file the application if:

- the birth parents have consented to the child's placement for adoption and not withdrawn that consent;

  AND

- given consent to the making of an adoption order;
- the parents have not been given leave of court to oppose the adoption order.

Usually staff from your adoption agency will assist you with making the application and providing some of the accompanying documents.

You will almost certainly require legal advice and assistance if the birth parents have been given leave to oppose the adoption order and/or have applied for a contact order to be made with the adoption order. It is vital to consult a solicitor who has experience in adoption law.

HELPFUL GUIDE

Adoption: A guide for court users (Form A20)
Available at www.adoption.org.uk/information or
www.hmcourts-service.gov.uk

If the child is looked after by the local authority, then it should pay your legal costs. If you are on a very low income, you may be eligible for public funding to pay legal costs; your solicitor will advise about this.

If you do not wish your identity to be disclosed to the birth family, you can ask the court for a serial number which replaces your name and address on the application and court documents.

The following documents must be filed at the court, along with your application. The application must be filed in triplicate on a standard court form. If the application is opposed by the birth parents, you must also file a "statement of facts" in triplicate (see below).

- your marriage or civil registration certificate (unless you are a single adopter)*

- a decree absolute, if you have been divorced, or dissolution of civil registration certificate*

- a copy sealed by the court of the placement order or section 19 consent that the child is subject to

- if you are non-agency adopters (usually in step-parent and intercountry adoptions), any documents available to you that show the birth parent/s have consented to the adoption

- your adoption agency (or local authority, for step-parent or intercountry adoptions) will file an Annex A report at the court when the court notifies the agency of your application.

There is a court fee for the application. Currently, the fee is £30 per child in the Magistrates Court and £160 per child or sibling group in the County Court and High Court. If the child has been placed for adoption by an adoption agency, which is supporting the application, the agency is expected to pay the court fee (Adoption Support Services Regulations) if it supports the adoption.

If the birth parents consent to the application for an adoption order, the court will appoint a Reporting Officer. This person interviews the birth parents, ensures that they give their consent unconditionally and with full understanding, and if so, witnesses their written consent.

---

*These must not be photocopies.

Speeding up the court process in adoption

The DfE has been working with the Department for Constitutional Affairs (which is responsible for courts in England and Wales) to speed up the legal process of adoption. This is being achieved with several initiatives, including: increasing the number of judges dealing with family work; making better use of judges and magistrates with expertise in adoption; finding new ways to manage adoption cases and thus reduce delay; and improving communication between everyone involved in the court adoption process.

Adoption Centres have been established in England and Wales to centralise all adoption work from county courts. The centres have specialist judiciary and staff who are experienced in adoption proceedings. If you have made an application to a County Court which is not an Adoption Centre, the application will be transferred by the court.

Section 1 of the Adoption and Children Act 2002 requires the court to timetable adoption proceedings quickly, because delay is likely to be prejudicial to the child's welfare.

What happens if the birth parent/s are given leave to oppose the adoption?

If the birth parents oppose the application:

- You are required to ask the court (via your solicitor if you have one) to dispense with the birth parents' consent. This is done by filing with your application a "statement of facts" (in triplicate) setting out the child's past and current circumstances and the reasons why you believe the legal grounds for dispensing with parental consent are met. The statement of facts should be prepared by your solicitor or by the Legal Department of the local authority if the child is in care. Legal grounds for dispensing with consent must be proved to the court. The grounds (section 52 Adoption and Children Act 2002) are:
    - the parents cannot be found; or
    - the parents are incapable of giving consent; or
    - the welfare of the child requires the consent to be dispensed with.

- If a parent is given leave of court to oppose the adoption order, the court will appoint a **Children's Guardian** to examine all aspects of the adoption order application and to prepare a report advising the court as to whether the adoption order is in the best interests of the child, or whether some other order might be better. The Guardian will interview you, the birth parent/s, the social workers and, probably, the child. The Guardian will also undertake any other investigation considered necessary or ordered by the court.

When must adopters attend court proceedings and why?

There are two types of court hearings: "directions hearings" and the final hearing for the adoption order application. You may not be required to attend directions hearings, but it is usually best to do so, subject to your solicitor's advice. You are required to attend the final hearing. You should bear in mind that birth parents will also be entitled to attend the hearings and you may need to consider with your solicitor and agency what precautions may need to be taken to avoid meeting them.

Directions hearings There may be several brief court hearings before the final hearing at which the application for the adoption order is decided. These directions hearings enable the court to advise you and/or your solicitor (and other parties) about procedural and evidential matters which need to be resolved; for example, the appointment of a Children's Guardian; the date by which the adoption agency must submit the Annex A report; and a mutually convenient date for all parties and witnesses to attend the final hearing.

Final hearing You are required to attend this hearing because you are the applicant/s and the court will not hear an application in your absence. You will be represented in court by your solicitor. The judge or magistrates will want to see you in person. If the application is opposed, the judge or magistrates will also want to see the birth parents. The judge or magistrate will hear oral evidence and then consider all the circumstances of the case (including the content of the Annex A and Guardian's report) and will decide if the adoption order is in the best interests of the child.

Other parties

Local authority If the child is subject to a placement order or section 19 consent, or the local authority has prepared a report in a non-agency adoption (step-parents or relatives), the local authority is a party to the adoption order proceedings. The local authority solicitor and at least the child's social worker (also sometimes a manager or other social work witness) will attend court and participate in the hearing – presenting to the judge the local authority's views on your application.

Birth parents Those with parental responsibility will automatically be parties to the proceedings. Sometimes the court will make a father without parental responsibility a party, and he is then entitled to legal representation in court.

The child Sometimes the court makes a child a party to the proceedings so that he or she can be legally represented. The child's solicitor will usually be instructed by the Children's Guardian. Unless the guardian has asked the court to excuse the child's attendance, he or she will be required to attend court, but only if the judge has decided that adoption is in the child's best interests and so that the adoption order can be made with the child present. Therefore, the child is not required to attend court to hear the evidence or the legal arguments for and against your application.

Where your identity is not known to the birth parent/s, and if you and the birth parent/s are both attending the final hearing (or any directions hearing), your solicitor should ensure that arrangements are made by the court so that you arrive at separate times and do not appear in the courtroom at the same time.

At what age will my child be permitted to read his or her children's services records?

Your child may be able to read information held about him or her, or any records, depending on the child's age and level of understanding. Adoption agencies are generally moving towards a more open approach and current practice is certainly to share information. Each case is determined on an individual basis. Of course, your child will not have access to information held about any third party involved. When your child is 18, he or she will be able to access information held about themselves by the agency and the court.

NMS 2.1 requires that:

The adoption agency is active in its efforts to obtain for the child clear and appropriate information from the birth parents and birth family about:

- themselves and the child's birth and early life;

- why the child could not remain with their birth parents;

- why the child was placed for adoption;

- health issues of the birth parents and their children;

- the views of the birth parents and birth family about the adoption and contact; and

- up-to-date information about themselves and their situation.

Local authorities must specify in the Adoption Placement Plan before the placement the dates on which the later-life letter and the child's life story book will be given to you.

What information can we and should we have?

You are entitled to read information about yourself that is held by the agency under Data Subject Access Rights, except information provided by your referees, unless they consent to disclosure. The agency must also make accessible to you information about your adopted child.

Statutory Adoption Guidance 4.24 states that, when considering a match between prospective adopters and a child:

It is unacceptable for agencies to withhold information about a child and provide a picture that bears little relation to the reality. The information provided must include full details of the child's background. This includes the history of any abuse or neglect and/or sexualised behaviour on the part of the child, their history in care, including the number and duration of placements, education and progress (or difficulties), behaviour and comprehensive information about physical and mental health and development and the implications for the future.

What is the legal position if I/we decide that we no longer wish to care for a child placed with us by an agency for adoption? Can I/we return the child to the agency?

If you are prospective adopters and the child is living with you *before* an adoption order is made, you have parental responsibility for him or her shared with the local authority and birth parents. You can ask to return the child to the agency, which is obliged to receive the child. If the child leaves, you will no longer have parental responsibility.

Once an adoption order is granted, you, as adoptive parents, become the child's legal parents, and have sole parental responsibility for the child, until and unless a subsequent adoption order is granted to other people.

The legal status of an adopted child is the same as a child living with birth parents – the adopted child is regarded in law as having been born to the adopters. Once adopted, the child cannot be "returned to the adoption agency", and the adoption agency is not obliged to receive the child into its care. However, you can ask the local authority where you live to accommodate the child – he or she will then become "looked after".

Like any family, you can ask the local authority children's services department to assist and advise you in caring for the child, and if you feel you cannot cope with the child at home, you can ask for the child to be accommodated by the local authority. The decision as to whether accommodation is in the best interests of the child rests with the local authority. That accommodation will be in foster care or a children's home for as long as is considered necessary. Like any parents, you will be asked to participate in decision-making about your accommodated child, and you may ask for his or her return.

However, if the local authority considers the child to be at risk of significant harm, attributable to the standard of your parental care, or that the child is beyond your parental control, it may institute court proceedings for an emergency protection order or care order. As parents, you will be entitled to legal aid automatically.

Money matters

How much does it cost to get an adoption order?

Court fees: These currently range up to £160 in the County Court and High Court, depending upon the court where the adoption application is filed.

If the child is being adopted from local authority care and the local authority supports the application, the expectation is that it will pay the court fee if it supports the adoption.

Legal costs: If the birth parent/s oppose the adoption, you will also be liable for your solicitor's costs in advising and representing you in court. Again, if the child is being adopted from local authority care and the local authority supports the application, it is expected to meet the adopters' legal costs. If you are on income support or a very low income, ask your solicitor about public funding of your legal costs.

Other costs: Adoption agencies can and usually do charge a fee for an assessment or prospective adopters of children from overseas. If you are adopting from overseas, you will also incur travel expenses and may have to pay additional fees to authorities in the child's country of origin (see Section 1 for more details) and fees to the DfE and the local authority in supervising the placement.

What types of financial assistance may be available to help with our adopted child?

For children adopted from care, financial help may be available during placement of the child and before the adoption order is granted.

Different types of financial support may be available to prospective adoptive parents. This support is based upon the financial need and resources of the adoptive family and upon the particular costs the family will incur as a result of being introduced to the child, and the child going to live with them. Each local authority will assess the family's need in order to determine if support is necessary. The types of support *may* include:

- travel expenses for introductions to the child;
- travel expenses for the child's contact with his or her birth family;
- costs of beds, wardrobes, etc (for example, if you are adopting a sibling group);
- special equipment and house adaptations;
- payment for loss or damage;
- ongoing financial support, which may be paid before an adoption order. This is likely to be paid less child benefit and tax credits and should normally not exceed what would be paid to foster carers of the child;

HELPFUL ORGANISATIONS

Children and Family Courts Advisory and Support Service (CAFCASS)

Practitioners who provide advice to courts about the welfare of children. CAFCASS administers the children's guardians service.

6th floor, Sanctuary Buildings
Great Smith Street
London SW1P 3BT
Tel: 0844 353 3350
Email: webenquiries@cafcass.gov.uk
www.cafcass.gov.uk

Child Law Advice Line

0808 802 0008

Community Legal Service

A government initiative designed to ensure that everyone has access to quality legal advice and information, including by funding legal costs for those on a very low income without significant capital. The service can be provided by Citizens Advice Bureaux (CABs), solicitors' firms and legal advice centres that have been awarded the Community Legal Service Quality mark.

You can find the *Community Legal Service Directory* at your local library. It lists all the law firms and advice centres which have the Quality Mark, and indicates whether firms offer free advice or if they charge.

Tel: 0845 345 4345 for advice and information about CLS providers or about the CLS directory.
www.legalservices.gov.uk

Coram Children's Legal Centre

Specialises in law and policy affecting children and young people. Produces information sheets and booklets. In addition to policy and campaign work, CLC also provides an advice and information service (free and confidential legal advice).

Helpline: 0808 802 0008 (free legal advice)
www.coramchildrenslegalcentre.com

Family Rights Group

A national organisation that advises families who are in contact with children's services, about the care of their children.

The Print House
18 Ashwin Street
London E8 3DL
Tel: 020 7923 2628
Advice line: 0808 801 0366
Email: advice@frg.org.uk
www.frg.org.uk

www.family-solicitors.co.uk

An online information service that provides advice and specific information about adoption, and lists solicitors who specialise in adoption and other aspects of family law.

www.compactlaw.co.uk

An online legal and information service that provides specific information about adoption law.

- other financial support that might include respite care, emergency support, domestic help, therapy for the child, or other costs involved during the placement.

If the child is less than five years old, placed singly and without significant special needs or disabilities, it is unlikely that most of these expenses will be met by local authorities or that ongoing financial support will be paid.

State benefits for a child's special needs (such a Disability Living Allowance or Carer's Allowance) may be available to adopters from placement. Child benefit is payable from the date of placement for the time of adoption, and tax credits can be claimed.

TERMS YOU MAY NEED TO KNOW

Fostering allowance – financial support payable by local authorities to foster carers (not to prospective adopters). There are nationally recommended rates for foster carers but these do vary considerably between local authorities.

Settling-in financial support – most local authorities will make available a settling-in grant. This is a discretionary grant and you can ask your social worker how to apply for it.

Is regular financial support available after an adoption order?

Regular financial support can be paid on a weekly or monthly basis to adoptive parents before and after the adoption order is granted. This allowance is permitted under the Adoption Support Services (Local Authorities) Regulations 2005 (and equivalent regulations in Wales). Financial support is designed to facilitate adoptions of children who might otherwise not be adopted, due to the financial cost to the adopters. The allowance is not taken into account for income-related benefits and income tax.

According to the Adoption Support Services Regulations 2005, financial support may be paid if one or more of the following circumstances exist:

- the child has not been placed with the adoptive parents for adoption, and financial support is necessary to ensure that the adoptive parents can look after the child if placed with them;

- the child has been placed with the adoptive parents for adoption, and financial support is necessary to ensure that the adoptive parents can continue to look after the child;

- the child has been adopted, and financial support is necessary to ensure that the adoptive parents can continue to look after the child;

- the local authority is satisfied that the child has established a strong and important relationship with the adoptive parent before the adoption order is made;

- it is desirable that the child be placed with the same adoptive parents as his or her brother or sister (whether of the full blood or half blood) or with a child with whom he or she has previously shared a home;

- the child needs special care which requires a greater expenditure of resources by reason of illness, disability, emotional or behavioural difficulties or the continuing consequences of past abuse or neglect;

- on account of the age, sex or ethnic origin of the child it is necessary for the local authority to make special arrangements to facilitate the placement of the child for adoption.

The amount payable as regular financial support is determined by the local authority, which takes into account the adopters' financial resources and commitments (not including the value of their home).

Financial support paid after adoption must not include any element of fee or reward which the carers were receiving as foster carers of the child. However, the exception to this is when foster carers wish to adopt a child whom they are fostering. They may continue to receive financial support, which includes a reward element for two years and, in some situations, for longer, after an adoption order.

Adopters receiving regular financial support must inform the local authority of changes in their financial or other circumstances and supply an annual statement of their finances. Financial support must be reviewed annually.

Payment of financial support will not affect other benefits you receive, such as Income Support, except the element for the child. Contact the Benefit Enquiry Line (0800 882 200) for more information.

What about a lump-sum payment?

Instead of regular ongoing financial support, the local authority may agree with you to pay you a single lump-sum payment or a series of lump-sum payments, to meet specific assessed needs.

Can I apply for financial support after an adoption order?

Yes. The Adoption Support Services Regulations 2005 provide that adoptive families can ask for their need for adoption support, including financial support, to be assessed at any point before or after the adoption order until their child is 18 and ceases full-time education or training. Local authorities have a duty to do an assessment if asked. You would need to apply to the local authority which placed the child with you unless it is more than three years since the adoption order. If this is the case, you need to apply to the local authority where you live. However, if you were receiving regular financial support before the adoption order and continue to receive it, the responsibility for that financial support continues with the placing agency, wherever you live.

Your entitlements regarding financial support

There is currently a lack of consistency among local authorities in assessment and payment of financial support.

However, local authorities are *required* to:

- consider if financial support should be paid;
- inform adopters about available financial support;
- give adopters written notice of the proposed decision about financial support;
- hear representation from adopters about financial support;
- review the financial support annually.

If you believe your needs have not been fairly assessed or if you have other complaints about the adoption support, use your local authority complaints procedure in the first instance. If you still are not satisfied, you may contact your Local Authority Ombudsman.

Statutory Adoption Guidance 9.20 states that:

> 'The placing local authority is responsible for the continued payment of financial support agreed before the adoption order is made. It is important that this provision is not misinterpreted as justification for a decision to pay ongoing financial support for a period linked to those years from the making of the adoption order. Any decision on the provision of support must be based on the needs and resources of the child and family. This applies equally to a decision about the period for which financial support is payable.'

Other benefits

The local authority cannot duplicate the financial help you might receive from state benefits (and tax credits). Other types of benefits may be payable to adoptive parents by the Benefits Agency, as for any child in their family, under certain circumstances. These benefits are not automatically payable if you have an adopted child with physical, mental or emotional difficulties. However, it is worth knowing which benefits exist and are available in case you require financial support at some point in the life of your adopted child. You will need to find out which are means tested. These benefits currently include:

- **Disability Living Allowance (DLA)** Some families now receive DLA for children who have attachment difficulties. This is the exception, not the rule, however, and you will have to apply to your local benefits office in order to receive this payment.

- **Carer's Allowance** Adoptive parents, like all parents of children with disabilities, may be eligible for Carer's Allowance *in addition* to Disability

Living Allowance, as long as one parent is not in full-time employment or earning more than £50 per week (irrespective of the partner's income). Many adoptive parents (usually mothers) are unable to take jobs because the needs of their children are so immense and because childcare arrangements are generally unable to meet the children's specific needs.

HELPFUL RESOURCES

For information about benefits, contact:

- the Benefit Enquiry Line 0800 882 200;

- your local post office (applications and information about various available benefits);

- your local Citizens Advice Bureau (offers advice and information) – check your local phone book for the Bureau nearest you;

- your local authority's welfare rights department (usually located within social services);

- *Community Care* magazine – www.communitycare.co.uk – click on 'Directory'.

Am I entitled to leave during the adoption of my child?

Yes – both statutory and adoption leave and pay and also statutory paternity leave and pay are now available (see Section 1).

Benefits provisions of the Carers and Disabled Children Act 2000

If your child has a physical or mental disability as defined by this Act, then you or your child may be eligible for:

- direct payments to 16- and 17-year-old young people who have a disability;

- direct payments to carers to meet their own assessed needs – this may mean that parents of a disabled child could receive a direct payment, rather than use the services provided by the local council, perhaps because they think existing services are not suitable or appropriate for their child.

Contact your local Benefits Agency for more information about these benefits and see Section 4.

Schooling and education

3

In this section

→ gain a general overview of the types of problems some adopted children may have in school

→ learn how schools can meet the needs of children who have difficulties

→ understand the process of obtaining special educational provision for your child

→ find out about current government initiatives and regulations to help you understand what support and services your child may be entitled to at school

→ find organisations and resources that can help you support your child at school and help you obtain the services that meet his or her specific needs

Introduction

Going to school is one of the main activities of childhood. Schooling not only teaches children academic skills, but also provides essential lessons in identity formation, relationship building and socialisation. Many adopted and fostered children have **learning difficulties** that may affect their ability to learn and/or their ability to socialise successfully with other children. According to the Department for Education, 'learning difficulty' means that '... the child has significantly greater difficulty in learning than most children of the same age; or the child has a disability which needs different educational facilities from those that schools generally provide for children of the same age in the area'.

Learning difficulties include apparent physical disabilities (such as motor disabilities, deafness or blindness) as well as less apparent difficulties, such as dyslexia, slow learners or "emotionally vulnerable" children.

In some cases, "emotionally vulnerable" children may be identified as having "**emotional/behavioural difficulty**" (EBD). This is defined by the SEN (Special Educational Needs) Code of Practice as 'a learning difficulty that requires special education provision'.

Some children may not be officially "identified" as having either of these difficulties, but may nevertheless have problems with academic and/or social skills at school.

It is important that adoptive parents recognise the possibility that their children may have difficulty at school. Your child will benefit if you are observant of his or her schoolwork and behaviour, and communicate openly with school staff. At the same time, it is also important to try to keep a "balanced" view of "normal" childhood behaviours and social interactions at school.

Adopters should be aware that, over the life of this handbook, there may be significant changes in the provision of education services and the organisation of schools and therefore in some of the information given in this chapter. Up-to-date information is available from the DfE website at www.dfe.gov.uk, or from your local authority.

What are we entitled to know about our child's educational history?

The Children Act 1989 requires local authorities to provide a **Care Plan** for every child in its care. The Care Plan should '...take account of the child's educational history, the need to achieve continuity, and the need to identify any educational need which the child may have, or carry out

HELPFUL BOOKS

... to inform educational and social work professionals about the impact of emotional trauma on a child's ability to learn:

Attachment, Developmental Trauma and Executive Functioning Difficulties in the School Setting by Marion Allen, Family Futures, 2008
Provides strategies and interventions to manage behaviour and establish an environment which will enable children to achieve their personal and academic potential.

Education: A foster carer's handbook by Barry Dixon, National Teaching and Advisory Service, 2008
A guide giving clear basic information about the education system.

Inside I'm Hurting: Practical strategies for supporting children with attachment difficulties in schools by Louise Michelle Bombèr, Worth Publishing, 2007
Provides educational professionals with a much-needed classroom handbook of strategies, practical tools and the confidence for supporting children (who have experienced trauma) from an attachment perspective.

Learn the Child: Helping looked after children to learn by Kate Cairns and Chris Stanway, BAAF, 2004
Good practice guide on helping and supporting traumatised children and young people in their learning. A new edition will be available in 2012.

Stop Wasting my Time! Case studies of pupils with attachment issues in schools with special reference to looked after and adopted children by Eileen Bebbington, Post Adoption Central Support, 2005
A helpful booklet which will help teachers understand attachment issues and create a calmer learning situation.

Supporting Children in Public Care in Schools: A resource for trainers of teachers, carers and social workers by John Holland and Catherine Randerson, Jessica Kingsley Publishers, 2005
A comprehensive training resource which provides guidance on how to support children who have faced loss as a result of significant changes in placement.

any assessment in respect of any special educational need'. Within the Care Plan, local authorities are required (according to Local Authority Circular (2000:13) to provide a **Personal Education Plan** (PEP) that '... ensures access to services and support; contributes to stability, minimises disruption and broken schooling; signals particular and special needs; establishes clear goals and acts as a record of progress and achievement.' The plan should:

- provide an achievement record (academic and otherwise);

- identify short-term targets; and

- establish long-term plans and aspirations.

Information about the child's education, including any special needs or statementing, should be given to you in the Child's Permanence Report.

Government guidance also requires that schools provide a "designated teacher" who oversees the education of looked after children. Statutory guidance, 'The role and responsibilities of the designated teacher for looked after children', makes clear that a child placed for adoption should be treated in the same way as any other looked after child for the purpose of school admission priority arrangements and in relation to the designated teacher's role. The statutory requirements change once the child is adopted and is therefore no longer looked after. However, Adoption Guidance 5.9 states that 'schools and designated teachers will need to recognise that the child's educational, social and emotional needs will not change overnight because of the adoption order'.

To help ensure continuity in meeting your child's educational needs after placement with you:

- check that information is contained in the Child's Permanence Report;

- ask to review copies of your child's Care Plan and PEP;

- speak to your child's teachers and/or designated teacher within his or her current school; and share the PEP and other relevant information with new teachers, if your child is moving to a new school.

The following information for social workers outlines the details you should be informed about when considering your child's educational background and current needs.

HELPFUL BOOKS

Attachment in the Classroom: The links between children's early experience, emotional wellbeing and performance in school by Heather Geddes, Worth Publishing, 2006
Explores the significance of the relationship between the pupil, the teacher and the learning task, linking it to emotional development, behaviour and attachment experiences.

Nutmeg Gets into Trouble by Judith Foxon, BAAF, 2006
An illustrated story book which explores some of the problems adopted children may have at school.

Families need to be fully aware of the child's educational history and [to] have the opportunity to discuss this with appropriate professionals, and... to read and discuss educational assessments and statements... Formal liaison between education departments is crucial to ensuring that the necessary... information is exchanged and that, with the family's involvement, the most suitable school can be identified... Social workers have important roles to play in co-ordinating the efforts of all involved to meet the individual needs of both child and family.

S. Byrne, *Linking and Introductions*, BAAF, 2000, p.13

Should I tell the school/teachers about my child's background?

Whether or not you choose to share details of your child's background with school staff is your own choice. Some parents may fear that their child will be treated "differently" if teachers know he or she is adopted, or that other children will ostracise the child if they discover anything about that child's background.

You might find that sharing selected details with school staff will help them treat your child appropriately during certain portions of the school curriculum, such as studying family history or family trees.

If your child has significant academic or socialisation problems that affect his or her schooling, then you will most likely have to share some details of the adoption with school staff. Often, open communication with teachers will help them work with your child in an appropriate and helpful manner.

TERMS YOU MAY NEED TO KNOW

The local education authority or LEA is now sometimes referred to as the local authority. To avoid confusion, we have used the term education department or authority interchangeably, to distinguish it from the local authority as a whole, but where terms like named LEA officer are still current, we have retained them.

Independent school A school neither maintained by a local education authority (LEA), nor a grant maintained school, but registered under the Education Act 1944. Section 189 of the Education Act 1993 gives the conditions under which an independent school may be approved by the Secretary of State as being suitable for the admission of children with statements of Special Educational Needs (see www.dfe.gov.uk).

Individual Education Plan (IEP) A written document, prepared by school staff, which lists specific goals a child should aim to achieve during a named school term. The goals in an IEP can include educational achievements, as well as improvements in social skills. Parents and older children can participate in writing the IEP.

Learning Support Unit (LSU) A classroom provided to support persistently disruptive, violent or unco-operative pupils. The LSU may offer an alternative curriculum and may also offer individual counselling. The goal of the LSU is to enable students to return to mainstream school, if possible.

Learning Support Assistant (LSA) A person who helps children who are in mainstream school, but who require extra learning support. LSAs are not specially trained, but are supported by the teacher and sometimes by visiting specialists.

Named LEA Officer The person from the education department who liaises with parents about arrangements concerning their child's assessment and statementing process. The education department will inform parents of the Named Officer when it proposes to conduct a statutory assessment of the child.

Named Person A person whom the education department *must* identify when it sends parents a final version of their child's Statement of Special Educational Needs. (Ideally, this person may be appointed at the beginning of the assessment process so he or she can attend meetings with parents and can encourage parents to participate in the process.) The Named Person must be someone who can give the parents information and advice about their child's special educational needs. The Named Person should be independent of the education department and may be someone from a voluntary organisation or a parent partnership scheme.

Non-maintained special school Schools in England approved by the Secretary of State as special schools which are not maintained by the state, but charge fees on a non-profit-making basis. Most non-maintained special schools are run by major charities or charitable trusts (see www.dfe.gov.uk).

Special Educational Needs Co-ordinator (SENCo) A teacher, appointed by the head teacher, who co-ordinates the services required for all children in the school who have special educational needs. This person can serve as a liaison between parents and the education department.

Special school 'A school which is specially organised to make special educational provision for pupils with special educational needs and is, for the time being approved by the Secretary of State under section 188 of the Education Act 1993' (see www.dfe.gov.uk).

Statement of Special Educational Needs A written document that is prepared by the authority after assessing a child. The document outlines, in detail, the child's educational needs and proposes how those needs should be met (see p.83). The authority must review the statement every 12 months.

How do I choose a good school for my child?

In addition to the usual considerations you have when choosing a school for your child, you may also have to think about the following questions if your child has learning and/or emotional behavioural difficulties.

- Does this school have experience of dealing with learning difficulties or emotional/behavioural difficulties?

- Does this school have the physical and/or financial resources needed to address learning or emotional/behavioural difficulties?

- Does the school specifically state it can handle emotional/behavioural difficulties?

- Can I communicate easily and comfortably with teachers and with the head teacher?

- How large is the school? Smaller class size and higher teacher to student ratios may make a smaller school easier for some adopted children. A small school, however, may not have the financial and/or physical resources that your child might require.

Independent schools are not subject to LEA regulations regarding special educational needs (see below) as are state-supported schools. You may find that some independent schools offer specific resources for children with "special needs". You should ask the school for its definition of "special needs" – sometimes these are defined only as learning difficulties and do not include emotional/behavioural difficulties.

What are "special educational needs"?

"Special educational needs" (SEN) include a broad range of problems that affect children at school – from specific learning difficulties to emotional/behavioural problems and developmental problems. The Department for Education (DfE) provides the following definition of special educational needs:

A child is defined as having special educational needs if he or she has a learning difficulty which needs special teaching. A learning difficulty means that the child has significantly greater difficulty in learning than most children of the same age. Or, it means a child has a disability which needs different educational facilities from those that schools generally provide for children of the same age in the area. The children who need special…education are not only those with obvious learning difficulties… [but also] those whose learning difficulties are less apparent, such as slow learners and emotionally vulnerable children.

HELPFUL RESOURCES

Bullying involving Children with Special Educational Needs and Disabilities, published by DCSF, 2008, available at www.anti-bullyingalliance.org.uk/pdf/SEN

Safeguarding Disabled Children: Practice guidance by M. Murray and C. Osborne, London: DCSF, 2009

The Social Care Needs of Children with Complex Health Care Needs by R. Marchant, M. Lefevre, M. James and B. Luckock, Social Care Institute of Excellence, London, 2007

An official definition of SEN is provided by the Code of Practice (1994) of the Education Act 1993. Identifying and addressing special educational needs should occur in three distinct phases, according to the Code of Practice:

1　Using existing school resources: if your child has difficulty at school, for example, difficulty following instructions, paying attention, or writing down information, the Code of Practice requires the school to address the problem using its existing resources, such as a classroom assistant or different teaching strategies.

2　If your child does not make progress, despite the support received from school, the school can consult external services (within education or other services) for specialist strategies or materials.

3　If progress is not made, then your child is entitled to a statutory assessment of SEN by the local authority education department. This usually involves your child completing a series of tests administered by an educational psychologist. The education department must comply with a request for an assessment unless it has already assessed the child within the last six months or if it decides an assessment is not necessary. Parents can appeal against this decision.

The authority is required to provide a **Statement of Special Educational Needs** for your child if:

• your child would be best served in a different mainstream school or by specialist resources within the same school; or

• your child would benefit from specialist and frequent support; daily LSA support; special equipment; regular involvement of non-educational agencies; or placement in a day or residential special school.

If your child is assessed for a statement, it does not necessarily mean that the authority will issue a statement. For example, it may find that your child's needs can be met within existing school resources. The authority must then issue a "note in lieu" to the parents and must also inform parents of their right to appeal against this decision.

Each authority is now also required to inform parents of its **"parent partnership" service**, in which a "named person" is identified to support parents whose child is undergoing the statementing process. Each authority should have a **named officer** who liaises with parents about statutory assessment and preparing a statement.

If your child receives a Statement of Special Educational Needs, the statement must be reviewed every year by you, the head teacher, a representative from the authority and any other person involved with your child at school. Older children may also participate in these meetings.

The current trend among education authorities in England and Wales is to educate children in mainstream schools whenever possible; to work co-operatively with other agencies and services (e.g. health and social services); to meet students' special needs; and to implement creative and cost-effective ways to address special educational needs within schools. At the moment, services for children with special educational needs vary widely among education authorities. If your child requires SEN services, therefore, you may have to communicate openly and frequently with your school and with your local authority to help your child obtain the services that will best meet his or her educational needs.

It may sometimes seem like you have to dig through endless layers of bureaucracy in order to obtain the services that will best meet your child's needs. But keep digging – it is the best way to make sure that the school and the local authority understand your child's needs and provide the resources required. It may also help pave the way for other adoptive families dealing with the school system.

The Government has proposed radical changes to the provision of services for children with special education needs. It issued a Green Paper, for consultation, in March 2011, *SEN and Disability*. It proposes, among other things, a single assessment process leading to a comprehensive Education, Health and Care Plan to replace, by 2014, the current statutory SEN assessment and statement. Parents will be given more choice and the ability to choose either mainstream or special school provision and there is a proposal for the option of personalised funding by 2014. You can find more information at www.dfe.gov.uk/education.

Understanding your child's entitlements to special education provision

SEN Code of Practice (2001) – provides schools and local authorities (LAs) with a framework for making decisions about various aspects of special educational needs – it provides general guidance, but does not dictate what LAs must do in individual cases. The Code of Practice was revised, based on consultation with the National Advisory Group on SEN, and came into force on 1 January 2002. Technically speaking, government circulars provide "guidance" and are not law, so parents should be aware that LEAs and/or SEN tribunals are not required by law to follow such guidance.

SEN tribunal – a judicial body to which parents can appeal for any of the following reasons:

- if the LA decides not to assess their child for SEN;

- if the LA assesses the child, but decides not to issue a statement of special educational needs;

- if parents disagree with the LA's decision about what SEN help the child needs;

- or if the LA tries to withdraw the child's statement, but the parents think the child still needs it.

The tribunal's decision is binding on the LA, regardless of the cost or resources required to meet the child's needs. The SEN tribunal is required to follow the SEN Code of Practice when making its decisions.

Government Circular 01/98 – This circular is entitled *Coverage of Behaviour Support Plans* and includes general guidance to LAs about providing support and assistance in schools for pupils with emotional/ behavioural difficulties. LAs are not required to follow this guidance, because it is not law. However, this information can give parents a general idea of the types of services the LA is expected to provide.

HELPFUL ORGANISATIONS

Contact your local authority to find out if it produces a Parents' Information Guide about schools in your area and their services, including special educational needs. Some LAs or councils also have a website that provides such information. Search on www.dfe.gov.uk/info/to find out if a site exists for your local area.

Information on special educational needs

Advisory Centre for Education (ACE)
Provides information about all aspects of state education, and helps parents who are dealing with schools or education authorities. Has a number of booklets and briefings available as free downloads.

Unit 1C, Aberdeen Studios
22 Highbury Grove
London N5 2DQ
Tel: 0808 800 5793 (advice line 2–5pm)
"Exclusion" information line:
0808 800 0327
www.ace-ed.org.uk

Caspari Foundation (formerly Forum for Educational Therapy and Therapeutic Teaching, FAETT)
Established in 2000, this organisation promotes educational therapy and therapeutic learning to help children who have emotional barriers that can impair learning. Provides courses for teachers, as well as consultations for children and their parents.

53 Eagle Wharf Road
London N1 7ER
Tel: 020 7704 1977
www.caspari.org.uk

Children in Scotland
Provides a national information and advice service for parents, professionals, children and young people living in Scotland who have questions about special educational needs.

5 Shandwick Place
Edinburgh EH2 4RG
Tel: 0131 228 8484
Email:
enquire.seninfo@childreninscotland.org.uk
www.childreninscotland.org.uk

Enquire
Scottish advice service for additional support for learning.

Helpline: 0845 123 2303
www.enquire.org.uk

Coram Children's Legal Centre, Education and Advocacy Unit
Provides advice and representation to children and/or parents involved in education disputes with a school or a local education authority. The Unit operates within the south-east of England. For education disputes outside this area, the Centre can provide advice, as well as negotiation and mediation services.

Tel: 0808 802 0008
www.coramchildrenslegalcentre.com

ContinYou
ContinYou is one of the UK's leading community learning organisations. They provide services and programmes in partnership with schools and other organisations for children and young people, particularly those from disadvantaged communities, to help young people identify, understand and overcome the educational barriers they face.

Unit C1, Grovelands Court
Grovelands Estate
Longford Road, Exhall
Coventry CV7 9NE
Tel: 024 7658 8440
Tel: 020 7587 5080 (London office)
www.continyou.org.uk

Department for Education (DfE)

Provides information for parents about all aspects of education and schools. The DfE website offers a Parents' Centre that provides specific and comprehensive information about SEN. Contact the DfE publications department to find out about specific information for parents, such as the SEN Guide for Parents, and for a copy of the Code of Practice.

DfE Publications
Tel: 0845 602 2260
Email: dfe@prolog.uk.com
www.parentcentre.gov.uk
www.dfe.gov.uk

Independent Panel for Special Education Advice (IPSEA)

A charity that aims to ensure that children with special educational needs receive the special education provision to which they are legally entitled. Provides free, independent advice; free advice on appealing to the Special Educational Needs Tribunal (including representation, if needed) and second opinions from professionals.

Hunters Court
Debden Road
Saffron Walden CB11 4AA
Advice line:
Tel: 0800 018 4016
www.ipsea.org.uk
Tribunal helpline: 0845 602 9579

The Institute for Arts in Therapy and Education

A college of higher education dedicated to in-depth theoretical and practical study of artistic, imaginative and emotional expression, and the understanding and enhancement of emotional well-being.

2–18 Britannia Row
London N1 8PA
Tel: 020 7704 2534
www.artspsychotherapy.org

National Association for Special Educational Needs (NASEN)

Promotes the education, training, advancement and development of people with special educational needs. Services to members include several regular publications and regional courses and conferences.

4–5 Amber Business Village
Amber Close, Amington
Tamworth
Staffs B77 4RP
Tel: 01827 311 500
Email: welcome@nasen.org.uk
www.nasen.org.uk

School Health Service

Identifies and assesses children who have physical, emotional or behavioural problems. It includes a named school nurse and paediatric doctors who have additional training to help with school services. The Health Service provides advice to LAs and offers specialist services, such as for enuresis (bedwetting) clinics, audiology services and for emotional difficulties. Contact your local authority to find phone numbers for your local School Health Teams.

SENAC – Special Educational Needs Advice Centre

Provides an independent advice, information and advocacy service for parents of children and young people with special educational needs.
Advice line: 028 9079 5779

Special Educational Consortium

Convened under the auspices of the Council for Disabled Children to protect and promote the interest of disabled children and children with special educational needs.

c/o National Children's Bureau
8 Wakley Street
London EC1V 7QE
Tel: 020 7843 1900
Email: sportic@ncb.org.uk
www.ncb.org.uk/cdc/sec.htm

Information about learning difficulties

British Institute for Learning Disabilities (BILD)

An independent, registered charity founded in 1972 to improve the quality of life for all people who have a learning disability. The institute conducts research into various aspects of learning disabilities, and provides information and services for people with learning disabilities, their families and for the professional community.

Campion House, Green Street
Kidderminster
Worcestershire DY10 1JL
Tel: 01562 723 010
Email: enquiries@bild.org.uk
www.bild.org.uk

DORE (formerly DDAT)

Helps people of all ages overcome their learning difficulties by improving their ability to learn, releasing their potential to live richer, more fulfilling lives. Provides assessment, consultation and treatment for children and adolescents who may have dyslexia, dyspraxia or attention difficulties.

www.ddat.co.uk

The Institute for Neuro-phsyiological Psychology

Established in 1975 to research the effects of central nervous system dysfunction on learning difficulties in children and on adults suffering from neuroses. The institute provides detailed information about this topic and about its services on its website or via post. Contact the institute for further information about its services and its fees.

Warwick House, 1 Stanley Street
Chester CH1 2LR
Tel: 01244 311 414
www.inpp.org.uk

The Mental Health Foundation

Provides information and support for people and families who have any type of mental health problem and/or learning disability. Included within the MHF is The Foundation for People with Learning Disabilities.

London office
9th Floor, Sea Containers House
20 Upper Ground
London SE1 9QB
Tel: 020 7803 1100
Email: mhf@mhf.org.uk
www.mentalhealth.org.uk

Scotland office
5th Floor, Merchants House
30 George Square
Glasgow G2 1EG
Tel: 0141 572 0125
Email: Scotland@mhf.org.uk
www.mentalhealth.org.uk
www.learningdisabilities.org.uk

Wales office
1 Langstone Business Park
Priory Drive
Newport NP18 2HJ
Tel: 01633 415 434
Email: Wales@mhf.org.uk
www.mentalhealth.org.uk
www.learningdisabilities.org.uk

Information about home schooling

Home Education Advisory Service (HEAS)

A UK-based national charity providing information and support for home education. Produces information, provides support for parents, and works with local authorities to monitor and inspect home education programmes.

PO Box 98
Welwyn Garden City
Hertfordshire AL8 6AN
Tel: 01707 371 854
Email: admin@heas.org.uk
www.heas.org.uk

Publications

Learn the Child: Helping looked after children to learn by Kate Cairns and Chris Stanway, BAAF, 2004 (new edition forthcoming, 2012).
A training resource for social workers, carers and teachers on helping looked after children to learn. It could also be helpful to adoptive parents.

Learning Disabilities in Children by Peter Burke and Katy Cigno, Blackwell Science, 2000.
Explains how learning difficulties are defined and examines their impact on family life. The book is aimed at those working in child welfare, social work and community care.

The Mental Health Needs of Looked After Children edited by Joanna Richardson and Carol Joughin, Gaskell, 2000.
Presents information on a range of mental health issues affecting children in care. Incorporates opinions and perspectives of children in the care system, and includes professional information and guidance regarding the young people's views.

Promoting Children's Mental Health within Early Years and School Settings
A booklet produced by the Department for Education (DfE) to help teachers and other people working co-operatively with health professionals, to promote children's mental health. It provides examples of mental health initiatives taking place within schools and gives advice on how to help children who are having difficulties or who have defined mental health problems.

DfE Publications
Tel: 0845 602 2260
www.dfespublications.gov.uk

Special Education Handbook: The law on children with special needs
Explains the process of obtaining a statement of special educational needs and various aspects of the statementing process. Available from the Advisory Centre for Education.

Special Educational Needs: A guide for parents
Available free from the Department for Education (DfE) publications section.

Special Educational Needs Update
A newsletter published by the DfE and sent to all schools, local education authorities, health authorities, children's services departments, and NHS Trusts in England. For more information contact the DfE.

Tel: 0845 602 2260
www.dfes/gov/sen/update.

Special Needs: A guide for parents and carers of Jewish children with special educational needs
Available from the Board of Deputies of British Jews.

Tel: 020 7543 5400

Websites

Center for Positive Behavioral Intervention and Support
www.pbis.org
Created by the US Department for Education to help schools implement and sustain positive behaviour-intervention programmes.

Department for Education (DfE)
Provides links to various government initiatives for raising standards in education, and provides a database of good practice programmes throughout the country.

Your child: physical and emotional needs

4

In this section

→ learn about the general effects of trauma and neglect on children

→ examine the emotional and physical difficulties adopted children may experience

→ find out how to access the services your child may need and how to ensure your child receives the help to which he or she is entitled

→ gather information about the organisations and resources which can help you and your child with particular difficulties

Introduction

Children in need of adoption and fostering will have experienced separation from their birth families. These children, *regardless of their age*, will be affected (to varying degrees) by that separation. In addition to the effects of separation and loss, many of these children may also have experienced varying degrees of trauma as a result of neglect and/or abuse.

Many of us are generally familiar with the *physical* impact of neglect and abuse on children. However, it is important to be aware that the *emotional* effects of early trauma may be less obvious, but equally profound. The repercussions of this trauma can deeply affect your child, no matter at what age you adopted him or her.

Today there are many resources and services to help children who have physical, emotional and developmental difficulties as a result of early trauma. The purpose of this section, therefore, is to give you a basic understanding of the possible needs your adopted child may have, so that you can find the services and information to meet your child's needs.

Varying degrees...what does it mean?

The phrase "varying degrees" applies to all of the problems discussed in this section. Every child is an individual and your adopted child may – or may not – experience the difficulties presented here. There are many factors that determine how extensively a child is affected by emotional or physical trauma. These include the age of the child when he or she experienced the trauma and the length of time the child experienced the trauma. Younger children are less likely to be affected as deeply as older children – but even children adopted as infants can show the effects of early trauma later in life.

It may be difficult for you – or for the professionals involved with your adoption – to determine exactly how much your child may be affected by past experiences and what needs your child may have now or in the future. But you will be able to help yourself and your child if you are aware of potential difficulties that may arise, and know where to seek appropriate help if you need it.

Possible effects of neglect and/or abuse on children

Abuse and neglect of children can take several forms. The word "abuse" commonly refers to a clearly identifiable event or series of events in a child's life, whereas "neglect" refers to an ongoing experience of deprivation. "Abuse", however, can sometimes be used to cover both situations, so it is important to be clear about what has actually happened to a child. A common image of children in the care system is of children who have been sexually or physically abused. Yet many of them are being looked after solely as a result of neglect of their basic needs and such neglect can sometimes damage a child more than individual episodes of abuse.*

Regardless of how it occurs, neglect and abuse are **traumatic events** for a child. You may often hear health professionals refer to children experiencing trauma or being traumatised – a word defined in medical circles as meaning 'an emotionally painful and harmful event that sometimes leads to long-term mental difficulties'. It is this trauma that creates the emotional wounds that may take many years (or even a lifetime) to resolve.

What information can I find from the child's health records?

Your child's social worker is required by law to give you full information in writing about your child when the agency first approaches you about a child (the Child's Permanence Report). This will include a summary of the child's health information by the medical adviser. The initial health assessment of your child will record physical and mental development, and will also indicate any issues that should be followed up. A copy of the health assessment report will be sent to your child's GP as well as to you. It is sensible to discuss this either with your GP or with the agency's medical adviser who may have carried out the assessment and who will in any case submit comments on it to the adoption court. The making of an adoption order does not prevent you from consulting your adoption agency and its medical adviser if you have any concerns about your child's health. You may also ask your GP to consult the agency on your behalf.

Your child's health assessment may include information about his or her birth parents. It is important to remember that this information, whether given or implied, must be treated as strictly confidential, privy only to yourselves as parents, to your child's GP, to the adoption court and, when he or she is older, to your child.

It is good practice for the medical adviser to meet with the prospective adopter to share all appropriate health information, to discuss the needs of the child with whom they are matched, and to provide a written report of this meeting.

---

* See D. Goldman, *Emotional Intelligence: Why it can matter more than IQ*, New York, Bantam Books, 1997, p.195.

What physical and/or developmental problems might we have to deal with?

Symptoms of neglect or abuse can include, for example, severe nappy rash, inadequate and unexplained weight gain or loss, withdrawn behaviour (or its opposite, indiscriminate displays of affection), unexplained bruises and a history of frequent visits to hospital accident and emergency departments. Health visitors, doctors, social workers, teachers and others involved with the child can initiate action on the child's behalf to deal with the situation, which for some children may include being looked after by the local authority. A child's physical and emotional development will often improve with placement in a secure and loving environment, although in many cases this will take months, or even longer.

There may be some physical and developmental problems which do *not* go away after the child is placed with you or which may take many years to overcome. Some of these difficulties, such as small size, can result from poor antenatal care, as well as neglect after the child is born. These are difficulties, therefore, that you may have to deal with as adoptive parents.

Physical problems

In addition to any diagnosed conditions the child might have been born with (e.g. Down's syndrome, asthma, other physical disabilities), the child may have general problems, such as small size (height and weight) for his or her age and a tendency to contract minor illnesses (such as colds or other types of infections) more frequently than other children. Some children may have problems with wetting and soiling (day and/or night), due to delayed physical development. It will be important for you to work closely with your health visitor and/or GP to help your child with these problems. Although these problems will improve over time, your child may never completely overcome some of them.

Developmental problems

Children who have been neglected do not develop the same "skills" as other children of their age. Neglected children, for example, may not learn how to talk or how to speak properly; they may be slow in learning how to walk or run, how to throw a ball, how to use the toilet, or how to eat properly. These are only a few of the skills a neglected child may not learn. The extent to which a child develops skills will differ with each individual and will also depend on the extent and time scale of the neglect.

What does "delayed" mean?

Your child's development may well be described as "delayed". It is often unclear whether this is due to the abuse and neglect they have suffered or whether their development would always have been slow. The term "delay" may indicate that eventually the child will catch up in their development. This may happen with all the good care which you are able to give. However, it may not – and you must be prepared for the fact that your child's development may always be delayed to some extent and in some aspects.

Possible developmental delays due to neglect can include:

- delayed language skills

- limited attention span

- delayed motor skills

- learning difficulties

- immature behaviour for his or her age

- immature behaviour when interacting with other children

- lack of self-esteem

- inability to control emotions (anger and joy)

Most children learn many of these skills and, with time, catch up to their age level when they are placed in a nurturing environment. If you are unsure of your child's physical and/or developmental status when he or she is placed with you, it may be helpful to arrange a visit to your health visitor or child development clinic for assistance. Some children may have learning difficulties resulting from developmental delay. Some of these may not be noticed until the child reaches school age.

Developmental delay: chicken or egg?

It may be difficult to determine whether or not a child's difficulties are caused by physical, developmental or emotional problems. If your eight-year-old son wets himself at school, for example, is this problem due to a delay in his bladder development, delayed emotional maturity, distraction by other people at school, or the distance he has to travel to use the school toilets? Sometimes, all of these factors contribute to a child's problems. Thus, many parents don't know where to look for help.

A good place to begin looking for help is from your GP and/or health visitor. Ask for information about the Child Development Clinic in your area and/or the local paediatric consultant. You can also contact your local health authority for information about child development services in your area.

What emotional and/or mental health problems might you have to deal with?

Problems the child may be born with

Neglected or abused children may have different types of health difficulties which are not a direct result of neglect or abuse; for example, congenital conditions such as heart disease. If such illnesses or conditions are already diagnosed in the child (or if there is an inherited problem that exists in members of the birth family but currently not in the child), you should be fully informed and given advice by social workers and medical advisers. In rare cases, adopted children can develop congenital conditions some time after their adoption. In such situations adoptive parents are advised to contact their adoption agency in the interests of members of their child's birth family.

The developing foetus can also be damaged before birth if the mother was a heavy smoker or drinker, took harmful drugs or neglected herself and her diet.

Foetal alcohol spectrum disorder (FASD)

This term is used to describe a wide range of disorders affecting children whose birth mother misused alcohol during pregnancy. They are also known as foetal alcohol syndrome (FAS) or foetal alcohol effects (FAE). It is not clear what level of alcohol use – including timing in the pregnancy, volume, frequency and duration – can trigger structural damage to the brain in unborn babies. Characteristics of foetal alcohol syndrome often include abnormalities of growth, a weakened immune system, and certain facial features. Children with some, but not all, of these characteristics are said to have foetal alcohol effects. Most babies with FASD will seem irritable, have trouble eating and sleeping, and may be sensitive to sensory stimulation. They may also have some level of developmental delay and learning difficulties at a later stage. FASD cannot be "cured", but with

HELPFUL ORGANISATIONS

NOFAS UK (National Organisation on Foetal Alcohol Syndrome UK)
Committed to helping individuals affected by FASD and providing specialist services.

16 Beaufort Park
London NW11 6DA
Tel: 020 8458 5951
Helpline: 08700 333 700
Email: nofas-uk@midatlantic.co.uk
www.nofas-uk.org

DrugScope
The UK's leading independent centre of expertise on drugs and drug use.

www.drugscope.org.uk

consistency, support and loving care, children can be helped to understand and live with their condition.

HELPFUL BOOKS

Children Exposed to Parental Substance Misuse: Implications for family placement edited by Rena Phillips, BAAF, 2004
A very informative anthology which looks at the effects of tobacco, drugs and alcohol on the foetus, the newborn and the infant, and the implications for family placement. Available from BAAF (Appendix 1).

Holding on and Hanging in by Lorna Miles, BAAF, 2010
Tracks Wayne's journey from first being fostered by Lorna when he was nine years old, having been neglected and affected by domestic abuse and parental alcohol and substance misuse, through nearly four years of family life in a therapeutic placement.

Problems resulting from abuse or neglect

Children needing adoption may experience a range of mental health problems that are a direct result of abuse and/or neglect. These difficulties can be emotional and/or behavioural, and may include poor self-image and self-esteem; overly aggressive and/or attention-seeking behaviour; inability to form genuine attachment relationships with other adults and/ or children; anxious or "vigilant" behaviour; indiscriminate physical contact with strangers; inability to concentrate; lack of sense of "personal space"; and self-injuring or self-stimulating behaviours (e.g. masturbation).

Attachment difficulties

This is one of the main problems for children who have experienced abuse, neglect and the trauma of separation. Attachment, briefly described, is the process of emotional bonding that occurs between infants and their main caregiver (usually mothers) during the first several years of life. During this period the infant learns many aspects of emotions and socialisation from his or her caregiver and forms a secure, loving relationship with that person.

So what happens in infants and children who do not have this connection with a main caregiver? Research now indicates that lack of physical contact, stimulation and communication with a main caregiver can inhibit the child from developing social behaviours (such as sharing, learning right and wrong, etc) which he or she would have learned from the caregiver. It is now known that this lack of contact also affects the growth and development of certain areas of the brain. This then leads to a lack of emotional development (such as knowing how to express emotions verbally, e.g. 'I feel sad'). Children who have not formed an attachment to a main caregiver(s) are described by health professionals as suffering from "attachment difficulties" (also described in professional diagnostic manuals as *Reactive Attachment Disorder*).

This guide provides only a brief description of attachment difficulties in children. The good news is that there is a growing body of literature and support to help parents and children. Current research shows, for example, that the physical development of the brain can occur throughout life, once the child receives the appropriate stimulation and attachment to a main caregiver.

The difficult news is that children don't overcome attachment difficulties overnight. It takes a lot of perseverance, patience and determination from parents to help children overcome such problems.

Post-Traumatic Stress Disorder (PTSD) is a condition that may affect children and adults who have experienced extreme physical or psychological trauma. Thus, children who have suffered intense abuse or neglect or witnessed severe violence or, in some cases, experienced a sudden removal from a loved carer or familiar environment, may have difficulties with PTSD.

People who have PTSD suffer recurrent memories of the traumatic stress, rather than being able to "integrate" the traumatic experience into the normal cycle of emotional recovery. When the flashes of traumatic memory occur, the body experiences the same physical and psychological stress as if the event were actually occurring. This leads to physical and behavioural reactions, such as increased heart rate and breathing, sweating, panic, nightmares, eating disorders, aggression and hyperactivity. When a child's body and mind are continually bombarded by such stress, it affects the child's ability to recover a healthy emotional state. The child's behavioural responses to the stress affect his or her ability to socialise, to learn (thus to attend school) and to participate in family life and other "normal" childhood activities. Children who suffer from PTSD should receive professional medical and psychological help.

Obtaining health services for your child

Health services for babies, children and adolescents are provided by a range of professionals in both hospital and the community. The health visitor has a helpful role in health promotion and in identifying the health care needs of under-fives and in helping to ensure access to the services necessary to meet those needs. Health authorities/boards are obliged, under section 10 of the Education Act 1981, to inform parents of children under five of any relevant voluntary organisation which could help with a childhood disability or learning difficulty. This means that health

HELPFUL BOOKS

Attachment, Trauma and Resilience by Kate Cairns, BAAF, 2002
Kate, her husband and three birth children have fostered 12 children who remain part of their family. She draws on the wealth of her personal and professional experience to offer a vivid glimpse into life with children who have experienced attachment difficulties, abuse and trauma, and shows in a range of everyday situations how the family responded.

Fostering Attachments: Long-term outcomes in family group care by Brian Cairns, BAAF, 2004
Brian, who, along with Kate Cairns and their three birth children, fostered 12 children, takes a less theoretical view to examine the process of parenting traumatised children and the benefits of family group membership in aiding learning and recovery.

Together in Time by Ruth and Ed Royce, BAAF, 2008
Ruth and Ed look back on their decision to adopt a boy with attachment difficulties, the fear that their family was falling apart, and their experience of music and art therapy.

authorities should keep information about local self-help groups, etc. in order to provide effective information services.

Every child born since 1992 has a **Personal Child Health Record** – make sure you obtain this from your social worker or voluntary agency. If this record cannot be located, ask your local health visitor or GP to arrange for a new one to be made for your child. There are often delays in securing health records of children who have had several moves from area to area or who have a complicated medical history including hospital treatment. You may need to encourage your GP or hospital to persist in chasing these records. Sometimes the child's change of name presents a barrier to be negotiated, and your adoption agency's medical adviser should be able to help you with this.

The Carer Held Health Record produced by BAAF is specifically designed for carers of looked after children who may have frequent moves, to supplement the Personal Child Health Record. It should be kept confidentially by adults caring for the child and should accompany the child when s/he moves.

Community health services for children – these services can include: audiology, child development assistance, occupational therapy, physiotherapy, school health services, services for children with a learning disability, and speech and language therapy, in addition to other services. Services may include a **Learning Disability Nursing Team** whose nurses have specialist training to work with children who have a learning

HELPFUL TRAINING COURSES AND BOOKS

Training Courses

It's a piece of cake? Parenting hurt children

This 8-part course devised by Adoption UK is available to adoptive and foster parents through local authorities. The programme is designed to help parents develop understanding and expertise in dealing with attachment issues and the effects of early trauma in children. Parents explore their own expectations and share new and creative parenting strategies. For more information, see Section 5.

Enhancing Adoptive Parenting: A parenting manual for use with new adopters of challenging children

by Alan Rushton and Helen Upright, BAAF, forthcoming 2012

This parenting manual is written for adoption support workers and intended to make practical and relevant advice available to the many struggling adopters. The programme aims to support the stability of the adoptive placement, to reduce the level of child problems, and enhance parenting skills and understanding, and improve relationships.

Leaflets, booklets, guides

Attachment Handbook for Foster Care and Adoption by Gillian Scholfield and Mary Beek, BAAF, 2006

A comprehensive book that describes different types of attachment, attachment formation and development, and how children can be helped to form new attachments in foster and adoptive families.

Attachment, Trauma and Resilience: Therapeutic caring for children

by Kate Cairns, BAAF, 2002

Offers a vivid picture of family life with children who have experienced attachment difficulties, loss, abuse and trauma and how the family responded.

Building the Bonds of Attachment by Daniel Hughes, Jason Aronson, 2006

Critically acclaimed book for those who strive to assist poorly attached children, which blends attachment theory, research, and trauma theory with general principles of parenting and family therapy to develop a model for intervention.

Connecting with Kids through Stories: Using narratives to facilitate attachment in adopted children by Denise Lacher, Todd Nichols and Joanne May, Jessica Kingsley Publishers, 2005

An accessible guide to family attachment narrative therapy for the parents of adopted or fostered children.

Fostering Attachments: Long-term outcomes in family group care

by Brian Cairns, BAAF, 2004

In a reflective account, Brian describes the daily realities of parenting children with challenging behaviours and the benefits of family group membership in aiding learning and recovery.

Trauma, Attachment and Family Permanence: Fear can stop you loving

edited by Caroline Archer and Alan Burnell, Jessica Kingsley Publishers, 2003

Draws on the programmes offered by Family Futures to explore the challenges faced by the professional or parent who seeks to promote family permanence. Brings together a rich selection of ideas.

disability. They can provide help, support and advice, such as developing relationship and life skills, and with continence and physical or sensory disabilities. Contact your GP or your local health authority for details of this service in your area.

Health Link Worker (usually a named health visitor or named school health adviser) can co-ordinate services needed by pre-school and school-aged children who require extra health care.

Looking after the emotional health of children in foster care and in residential care

In 1996, the National Children's Bureau undertook a three-year project to identify the mental health needs of children in foster or residential care. The study found that carers are concerned about the mental health of the children in their care and that there is a lack of mental health support for carers from local health authorities. As a result of recent studies in Glasgow, researchers have concluded that, 'A better understanding of the emotional and behavioural difficulties experienced by many looked after children is crucial if appropriate interventions are to be provided. The first step towards this is for every child entering care to have a comprehensive psychological assessment so their individual needs can be identified and met.'*

TERMS YOU MAY NEED TO KNOW

Attention Deficit Hyperactivity Disorder (ADHD) is an impairment of activity and attention control. The diagnostic features are inattention, over-activity (especially in situations requiring calm) and impulsiveness.

Children who have been neglected or abused often display anxious and hyperactive behaviour as a result of insecure emotional attachment. This behaviour may sometimes be interpreted as ADHD or ADD (Attention Deficit Disorder). There is a great deal of controversy about these conditions and whether children diagnosed with ADHD or ADD actually have attachment difficulties rather than ADHD/ADD. It is important to be aware of these issues if you need to consult health professionals about your child's behaviour (see Appendix 2 for ADD organisations).

Won't there be extra "emotional hurdles" for my adopted child as he or she grows up?

Yes. In addition to the possible problems with self-esteem and attachment mentioned earlier, children may have questions about their life history

---

* H. Minnis and C. Del Priori, 'Mental health services for looked after children: implications from two studies', *Adoption & Fostering*, 25: 4, pp 27–38.

HELPFUL ORGANISATIONS

Meeting your child's physical, developmental, emotional and/or behavioural needs

In addition to the post-adoption support services described in Section 5, the following organisations may provide information and assistance.

The Anna Freud Centre

A registered charity that provides services to families and children with emotional, behavioural, and developmental difficulties. The Centre also conducts research into the effectiveness of psychotherapy techniques and children's emotional development, including attachment. Treatment is provided to families based on need, not on ability to pay.

12 Maresfield Gardens
London NW3 5SU
Tel: 020 7794 2313
www.annafreud.org.uk

Association for Child and Adolescent Mental Health

An association for professionals of various disciplines who are involved with children. It arranges seminars and publishes professional journals. It does not provide an advice service.

39–41 Union Street
London SE1 1SD
Tel: 020 7403 7458
www.acamh.org.uk

Association of Child Psychotherapists (ACP)

A professional organisation for child psychotherapists in the UK. Recognised by the Department of Health as the body which accredits UK training in child and adolescent psychotherapy.

120 West Heath Road
London NW3 7TU
Tel: 020 8458 1609
www.childpsychotherapy.org.uk

British Association for Counselling and Psychotherapy (BACP)

Provides details of local counsellors and psychotherapists online.

BACP House, 15 St John's Business Park
Lutterworth
Leicestershire LE17 4HB
Tel: 01455 883300 (information)
Email: bacp@bacp.co.uk
www.bacp.co.uk

The British Association of Psychotherapists (BAP)

The training institution and professional association of psychoanalytic psychotherapists, analytical psychologists (Jungian) and child psychotherapists.

37 Mapesbury Road
London NW2 4HJ
Tel: 020 8452 9823
www.bap-psychoterhapy.org

Caspari Foundation (formerly Forum for the Educational Therapy and Therapeutic Teaching, FAETT)

Promotes educational therapy and therapeutic learning to help children who have emotional barriers that can impair learning. Provides courses for teachers, as well as consultations for children and their parents.

53 Eagle Wharf Road
London N1 7ER
Tel: 020 7704 1977
www.caspari.org.uk

The Centre for Child Mental Health

The aim of the centre is to expand awareness of emotional well-being and mental health of children. It conducts research in child mental health, provides information for parents, teachers, professionals and the public, and provides seminars by mental health professionals, covering a range of child mental health topics, including issues that affect adopted children.

2–18 Britannia Row
London N1 8PA
Tel: 020 7354 2913
Email: info@childmentalhealth.centre.org
www.childmentalhealthcentre.org

Institute of Child Health

Works in partnership with the Great Ormond Street Hospital to form the largest paediatric training and research centre in the UK. The hospital offers the widest range of paediatric specialists in the country.

30 Guildford Street
London WC1N 1EH
Tel: 020 7242 9789
www.ich.ucl.ac.uk

YoungMinds

A children's mental health charity committed to improving the mental health of all children and young people. Provides information and services, as well as advocacy work within government and professional organisations; conducts training and seminars for professionals; and conducts consultancy work to develop services for children.

Also provides **YoungMinds Parents' Information Service** (see Section 5) and **written information** for young people, parents and professionals, such as: Leaflets – *How can psychologists help children?, How can child psychotherapists help?, How can family therapy help my family?, Children and young people get depressed too*; Resource sheets – *ADHD, Education, Depression, Anxiety*; *YoungMinds* magazine.

Suite 11 Baden Place
Crosby Row
London SE1 1YW
Tel: 020 7089 5050
Tel: 0808 802 5544 (parents helpline)
Email: info@young.minds.org.uk

and about their birth family, to varying degrees. The way in which these issues affect your child may be influenced by the child's age at adoption and by the amount of contact he or she has with the birth family. Very young children usually happily accept the story of their adoption, but as they grow old enough to understand the concept of rejection, some children become anxious or withdrawn when adoption is mentioned. Extra sensitivity is required if this seems to be happening. Help is available with this kind of difficulty, so do not hesitate to seek it if you feel uncertain about how to handle it. These issues can affect a child's behaviour without you – or your child – realising it.

It is important to talk openly with your child about his or her life history, and to provide the facts, little by little, as your child becomes old enough to understand them. Many adoptive parents help their children talk about their life history using the life story book provided by their social worker (see Section 1). Talking about these events openly and in a positive manner will help your child understand his or her life history and come to terms with any difficult issues. There are many resources and organisations that can help both you and your child along the way.

Can I ask the local authority for help after I have adopted my child?

Yes. Many local authorities are trying to keep in touch with adopters, as all voluntary adoption agencies do, by offering a regular newsletter, workshops, social events, etc. However, even if you are not in contact with a local authority, you can ask for help. If it is more than three years since your child was adopted, you should approach the local authority where you live. Otherwise, you should contact the local authority which placed your child with you. The Adoption Support Services Regulations 2005 impose a duty on local authorities to assess your needs and that of your child for adoption support at any time during his/her childhood.

All local authorities in England are required to have a range of adoption support services in their area. These are:

- financial support;
- support groups for adoptive parents and adopted children;
- support for contact arrangements between adopted children and their birth relatives or other important people;
- therapeutic services for children;
- training, respite care and other services to help support the placement;
- counselling, advice and information.

You and your child have a right to have an assessment of your needs for adoption support by the local authority, either those listed above or any others, e.g. help in liaising with schools, help in talking with the child about adoption, etc. The local authority must prepare a written adoption support plan which sets out what it has assessed your support needs are and how it proposes to meet these. Guidance to the regulations states that local authorities must act reasonably in deciding whether to provide adoption support services following an assessment. However, it may not be possible to provide a service to meet every need. You may be able to complain about or challenge "unreasonable" decisions (see booklet *Understanding the Adoption Support Regulations* produced by Adoption UK).

Promoting the health and wellbeing of looked after children – revised statutory guidance

This was issued in November 2009. It is statutory on local authorities and, for the first time, also on primary care trusts and strategic health authorities. It applies in England only. It sets out a framework for effective joint working between these agencies and gives guidance on providing

HELPFUL GUIDES

What is a Disability?, by Hedi Argent, 2004. A guide for children which describes different disabilities and explains what they mean. Available from BAAF (Appendix 1).

an effective service for looked after children and their carers. For more information, search online for the title of the guidance or access it via www.dh.gov.uk.

There are currently proposals for massive changes to the way that health services are provided, with the possibility of a move towards GPs commissioning all services.

Is it more difficult to adopt a child who has a physical, mental or learning disability?

No. The process for adopting a child with a disability is the same as for any other child. Again, the main concern of the adoption agency will be that you are able to meet the specific needs of that child. Because a disabled child may place different and/or additional pressures on adoptive parents, there are many disabled children waiting for adoption. Many local authorities have recognised this problem and are trying to recruit adoptive parents for these children.

Under the NHS and Community Care Act 1990 and the Children Act 1989, children's services have a duty to assess the needs of a child with a disability. If you adopt a disabled child, you have the right to ask for your child's needs to be assessed by the children's services department and you also have the right to ask for an assessment for yourself – this will be under the Carers and Disabled Children Act. Once your child's needs have been assessed, the social worker will agree with you what services are to be provided.

These services could include practical assistance in the home; provision of recreational or educational facilities; home adaptations; travel, meals, and other assistance; a telephone and ancillary equipment. Other services may be provided under the Children Act but these may be discretionary. You will need to find out what is available from your local authority and you can contact the Contact a Family helpline for more information.

Will we be more likely to receive financial support if we adopt a disabled child?

According to the Adoption Support Services Regulations 2005, financial support may be paid if the child 'needs special care which requires a greater expenditure of resources by reason of illness, disability, emotional

HELPFUL ORGANISATIONS

If your child has a physical or mental difficulty

There are many organisations which support children with specific difficulties. Those listed here are "umbrella" organisations that provide general support regarding adoption and/or physical or mental difficulties.

Contact a Family

Provides information for parents on over 2,000 rare medical conditions, including information about support groups, and publishes a useful directory, *The CAF Directory of Specific Conditions and Rare Disorders* (in print and online). There is also a freephone helpline for parents seeking information regarding help for disabled children.

209–211 City Road
London EC1V 1JN
Helpline: 0808 808 3555 Monday–Friday, 10am–4pm
Tel: 020 7608 8700
Textphone: 0808 808 3556
Email: info@cafamily.org.uk
www.cafamily.org.uk

Council for Disabled Children

Promotes collaborative work between different organisations providing services and support for children and young people with disabilities and special educational needs. Offers a range of services, including consultancy, training, information, publications and conferences.

8 Wakley Street
London EC1V 7QE
Tel: 020 7843 1900
email: cdc@ncb.org.uk
www.ncb.org.uk/cdc/index

PUBLICATIONS

Every Child is Special: Placing disabled children for permanence by Jennifer Cousins, BAAF, 2006
This Good Practice Guide considers permanence planning for disabled children and recruitment and assessment of families. It highlights the changes that are necessary if more disabled children are to have the security of a permanent family.

The Family Business by Robert Marsden, BAAF, 2008
A story of the adoption of William, a little boy with cerebral palsy, by a middle-aged couple with three birth children.

Whatever happened to Adam? Stories of disabled people who were adopted or fostered by Hedi Argent, BAAF, 1998
This remarkable book tells the stories of 20 young disabled people and the families who chose to care for them. The book follows the children's life journeys from joining their new families, through childhood and adolescence and into preparation for adulthood. A powerful and timely reminder that adoption and fostering can be tremendously rewarding for disabled children and for their adoptive and foster families.

When your Child has Additional Needs: A guide to help and support for parents of a disabled child Contact a Family, 2007
An extremely useful online guide that gives pointers to the kind of help that is available when caring for a child with a disability, special need or disorder.

Child and Adolescent Mental Health Services: Everybody's Business

Produced by the National Assembly for Wales, outlines the 10-year programme to improve the range and quality of child and mental health services in Wales. Copies of the report are available from the Primary and Community Healthcare Division, Tel: 029 2082 3480 or from www.wales.gov.uk

Child and Adolescent Mental Health Services Innovation Projects

are being initiated throughout the United Kingdom to offer direct mental health services to children, as well as consultation, support and training for teachers, health visitors and social workers. Among the 24 projects currently underway are:

- **Scallywags** – a community-based programme in Cornwall to provide early intervention for young children with behavioural and emotional difficulties. More information available from
  Email: scallywags@cornwall.gov.uk
  www.cornwall.gov.uk/scallywags

- **Support Service for Looked After Children in Sheffield** offers a range of therapeutic work for children in foster care and residential units, with birth families, and for some, after adoption.
  www.nspcc.org.uk

Framework for the Assessment of Children in Need and their Families

These are guidelines, produced by the Department of Health in 2000, to help social work professionals assess looked after children and children moving to adoption. For more information contact the Department for Education or access www.dfe.gov.uk

The National Clinical Director for Children

has recently been appointed to oversee development of the Children's National Service Framework. This initiative is intended to co-ordinate all NHS plans for children's services. Child and adolescent mental health and emotional well-being is one of six key areas to be addressed by the framework. For more information, see www.dh.gov.uk

The National Mental Health Development Unit

was launched in April 2009 to provide national support for implementing mental health policy by advising on best practice to improve mental health and mental health services. Although it closed on 31 March 2011, all the publications and resources remain available online.
www.nmhdu.org.uk

Ensuring your child receives the care to which he or she is entitled

Current legislation regarding children in England and Wales promotes the provision of *co-ordinated*, quality health services for children. This legislation may support your case if you think your child is not receiving needed services. Copies of the legislation are available at www.dh.gov.uk/PolicyAndGuidance/HealthAndSocialCareTopics/ChildrenServices/fs/en

Children's Services Plans

These are broad strategic plans designed to co-ordinate all services for vulnerable children, such as Education Development Plans, Early Years Development Plans, and Behaviour Support Plans. Co-ordination of all plans required for vulnerable children will be provided by local councils, with the full participation of NHS organisations (required by the "duty of partnership" described in the Health Act 1999).

or behavioural difficulties or the continuing consequences of past abuse or neglect'. You will be "assessed" for any financial support for which you may be eligible. For more information about financial support, see Section 2 of this handbook.

Families of disabled children may also be entitled to additional support, such as mobility allowance or attendance allowance. For more information about these allowances, contact your local Benefits Agency.

Carers and Disabled Children Act 2000

Implemented on 1 April 2001, this is a government initiative launched in 1988 which requires local authorities to ensure that children with specific social needs arising out of disability or a health condition are living with families or in other appropriate settings in the community where their assessed needs are adequately met and reviewed. This Act gives local councils the power to provide certain services directly to carers following assessment, even where the person cared for has refused an assessment. People with parental responsibility for a child also have the right to an assessment.

Local councils also have the power to make direct payments to:

- carers to meet their own assessed needs (this includes 16- and 17-year-old carers);
- 16- and 17-year-old disabled young people;
- parents of a disabled child, to purchase services to meet the assessed needs of the disabled child and family.

Parents or young people may want a direct payment because they think that existing services do not meet their child's or their own needs, and they believe they can make better arrangements themselves.

Assessments are made with reference to both the Children Act 1989, and the Department of Health Framework for the Assessment of Children in Need and their Families (2000).

HELPFUL RESOURCES

Organisations and information to help adopted children and adults who were adopted as children

AAA–NORCAP – Adults affected by adoption

A self-help support group for all parties to adoption. It offers advice for members on searching and a research service. It can play an intermediary role for those seeking renewed contact. NORCAP maintains a successful Contact Register and publishes a newsletter three times a year.
112 Church Road
Wheatley
Oxon OX33 1LU
Tel: 01865 875 000
Email: enquiries@norcap.org.uk
www.norcap.org.uk

Talk Adoption

A free, confidential national helpline for young people up to 25 years old who have a link with adoption, whether adopted person, friend or relative.
Tel: 0808 808 1234
www.talkadoption.org.uk

The Who Cares? Trust

A registered charity that promotes services for children and young people in public care, those who have left public care, and those whose lives continue to be affected by their care experiences. The Trust ensures the opinions of those directly affected by care are heard in the planning and provision of services for them. Publishes the *Who Cares?* magazine.
Kemp House,
152–160 City Road
London EC1V 2NP
Tel: 020 7251 3117
Email: mailbox@thewhocarestrust.org.uk
www.thewhocarestrust.org.uk

To contact birth parents/relatives

The Adoption Contact Register for England and Wales

Office for National Statistics
The General Register Office
Adoptions Section
Smedley Hydro, Trafalgar Road
Southport
Merseyside PR8 2HH
Tel: 0845 603 7788
www.direct.gov.uk/gro

The Adoption Contact Register for Scotland
Birthlink

c/o Family Care
21 Castle Street
Edinburgh EH2 3DN
Tel: 0131 225 6441
www.birthlink.org.uk

General Register Office for Northern Ireland

Oxford House, 49–55 Chichester Street
Belfast BT1 4HL
Tel: 028 9151 3101
www.nidirect.gov.uk/gro

General and health resources for children and young adults

Citizens Advice Bureau Advice Guide

Online help from Citizens Advice on young people and various health matters, including sexual health, drugs and alcohol, contraception, medical treatment, self-harm, and much more. www.adviceguide.org.uk

Child and Adolescent Mental Health

The CAMH website provides a free and comprehensive source of information for young people, parents and professionals about a range of mental health difficulties and disorders that may be encountered during childhood and adolescence.
www.camh.org.uk

The Connexions Direct website

The Connexions Direct website has become part of Direct Gov Young People. All relevant content for young people can now be found on www.direct.gov.uk/en/ YoungPeople/index.htm.

Depression Alliance

Promotes greater understanding of depression to reduce the stigma associated with it. Produces booklet, *The Young Person's Guide to Stress*.

20 Great Dover Street
London SE1 4LX
Tel: 0845 123 2320
www.depressionalliance.org.uk

Scottish Health on the Web (SHOW)

Provided by the NHS in Scotland, this site provides general health information, contact details of all NHS Trusts, and links to other websites.
www.show.scot.nhs.uk

UK Youth

A leading national youth development charity which develops, promotes and delivers a range of innovative education programmes in partnership with a national network of organisations. They aim to enable young people to raise their aspirations, realise their potential and have their achievements recognised.
7 Heron Quays
Canary Wharf
London E14 4JB
Tel: 01425 672347
Email: info@ukyouth.org
www.ukyouth.org

YoungMinds

The UK's leading charity committed to improving the emotional wellbeing and mental health of children and young people and empowering their parents and carers.
YoungMinds parents' helpline:
0808 802 5544
www.youngminds.org.uk

For adoptive parents

In this section

→ identify and focus on your own particular needs as adoptive parents

→ consider some of the most common emotions adoptive parents encounter and why these feelings occur

→ find the resources, organisations and services that can help you help yourself through the various emotions of the adoption experience

Introduction

By its very nature, adoption is a process that has its ups and its downs. The first four sections of this book describe many of the procedural, financial and emotional pitfalls that can potentially turn a happy experience into a stressful and frustrating nightmare.

The experience of having a child, by birth or by adoption, is always a journey into the unknown – none of us knows if our expected child will have any physical or emotional difficulties. Yet, because adoption is a *process* of bringing a child into your home and family, you can be fairly certain you will encounter some degree of difficulty at some point along the way.

Acceptance is the first step to a "smooth" adoption

The first step in making the experience of adoption as smooth as possible is to accept that adopting a child is different from giving birth to a child. You will have to adjust your preconceptions and your expectations about parenthood and having children. We hope the resources and information provided in this guide will help you cope with the procedural and physical difficulties you might encounter. The emotional difficulties involved in adoption are a different battle altogether – these are the experiences that challenge you and change you. These are the experiences we discuss in this section.

Adoptive parents' needs are important too

Adoption focuses on meeting the needs of a child. But this does not mean we should ignore the needs of adoptive parents. After all, if you do not look after your own physical and emotional needs, you won't be able to provide much help to your child.

Yet, every adoption is an individual event and everyone responds differently to it. So while we can't predict every emotional response you'll have throughout your adoption – and thus offer "answers" to every difficulty – we can describe some *general* feelings that most adopters experience and offer some *general* advice. Although it is difficult to "avoid" having certain experiences and feelings throughout adoption, just being *aware* of the feelings you might have can often help you get through particular experiences more easily.

Let's take a minute to discuss some of the "lows" of the adoptive parent's emotional rollercoaster. Why would this be helpful? If you have not yet adopted, or only recently adopted, it can help you prepare to expect some of these "lows" and, hopefully, to be less surprised if you experience these emotions. If you have already adopted, perhaps reading about some of the most common emotions adoptive parents face as a result of common experiences of the adoption process will reassure you that other adopters have similar feelings. This can help bolster your confidence as an adoptive parent.

Assessing risk and resilience in prospective carers

Research is currently underway to develop effective tools that will enable social workers and others to assess the emotional and psychological resilience of prospective adoptive parents or foster carers. The intent of this research is not to further scrutinise carers, but to ensue that, as adoptive/foster parents, you are matched with a child whose emotional, psychological and/or physical demands will not exceed your abilities to meet such demands. Current studies include:

Attachment style interview (ASI)

This is a standardised assessment tool developed at Royal Holloway, University of London. It can be used to assess the characteristics of carers in terms of their quality of close relationships, social support and security of attachment style. It assesses particularly the adequacy of support and the carer's ability to access support. It should only be used by trained assessors. A number of adoption agencies are now training workers to use the ASI and are finding it useful.

The use of the Adult Attachment Interview: Implications for assessment in adoption and foster care by M. Steele, J. Kaniuk, J. Hodges, C. Haworth and S. Huss.

This research was conducted at the Anna Freud Centre in London. Researchers studied the use of the Adult Attachment Interview (AAI) in assessing attachment in a group of parents who voluntarily adopted children with developmental delays. The AAI is commonly used in researching parent–child relationships, but has not previously been used in the assessment of carers. Contact the centre at www.annafreudcentre.org for more information (see Appendix 2).

Feelings and emotions adoptive parents commonly encounter throughout the adoption experience

"Instant" parenthood

Despite the months (perhaps years) of planning for your adopted child, it is difficult to be fully prepared for the child's arrival in your home. You can easily prepare for your child's physical needs. But being ready for your and your child's emotional responses (no matter what age child you have adopted) is altogether different. This is particularly true for individuals or couples who have not parented a child before – either born to them,

HELPFUL RESOURCES

Parents are Linked (PAL)

This service, co-ordinated by Adoption UK, links people who have particular questions about adoption with people who can provide useful information based upon their own experiences. The service is available to Adoption UK members. As a member, you can phone Adoption UK, register your question(s) with the PAL database, and then be matched with someone who may be able to help you. For more information, contact Adoption UK (see Appendix 2).

fostered or adopted. The first few months after the placement can be a time of joy, but may also bring feelings of guilt, depression, perhaps even panic. The question, 'Have we done the right thing?', might enter your head more than a few times after the child is first placed with you or after the adoption goes through.

It is important, at this stage, to remember you are a new parent or new to parenting this child and have taken on an immense challenge. You may find it helpful to share your true feelings with others – especially with other adoptive parents. It will also be important to give yourself "respite" time away from your child in order to "rest and recoup" from the stresses of parenting an adopted child.

"Sharing" your child

When your child is finally placed with you, it is common to want to immerse the child in your family life – in a sense, to make the child "your own". It can be difficult, at this time, to continually remind yourself that your child is the focus of the adoption process and that you might have to endure some experiences (such as visits with foster carers and/or birth parents) that you may not enjoy, but which may be in the best interests of your child. It can be painful, for example, to see your newly adopted child run to his or her former foster carers' arms for comfort, or to feel your child reject you in favour of other people he or she has known previously. Moreover, children who have attachment difficulties (see Section 4) are experts at manipulating other adults to their own advantage, while rejecting you in the process. When your child is first placed with you, you may feel surprised, confused and frustrated by such experiences.

"Attachment? What attachment?"

There will be times when you may have to face the issue of "love" for your child. Do you "love" him or her? Or do you feel sympathy, empathy, even "caring" and responsibility, rather than unconditional love? You will not be the first adoptive parent to ask yourself these questions. These

HELPFUL BOOKS

Books about attachment difficulties and parenting children who have attachment difficulties (see also Section 4)

Attachment Handbook for Foster Care and Adoption
by Gillian Schofield and Mary Beek, BAAF, 2006

**Attachment Theory, Child Maltreatment and Family Support:
A practice and assessment model** by David Howe *et al*, Macmillan, 1999

Attachment, Trauma and Resilience: Therapeutic caring for children
by Kate Cairns, BAAF, 2002

Building the Bonds of Attachment by Daniel A. Hughes, Jason Aronson
Inc, 2006

First Steps in Parenting the Child Who Hurts: Tiddlers & Toddlers
by Caroline Archer, Jessica Kingsley Publishers, 1999

Fostering Attachments: Long-term outcomes in family group care
by Brian Cairns, BAAF, 2004

Next Steps in Parenting the Child Who Hurts: Tykes & Teens
by Caroline Archer, Jessica Kingsley Publishers, 1999

A list of books of interest to families living with, and professionals
working with, children with attachment and behavioural difficulties is
available from Adoption UK (see Appendix 2).

feelings arise because many children who have been neglected or abused
do not exhibit any vulnerability – that is, they do not show any signs that
they really "need" parents. So, you may find it hard to love a child who
seemingly doesn't "need" you.

In addition, children with attachment difficulties may have behaviours that
make you feel rejected. These are times when your commitment as an
adoptive parent overrides all other emotions – you stick with it because
you believe in what you are doing, you believe in your child, and you
believe in your child's capacity to overcome his or her difficulties.

During these times, it is important to seek support from others – social
workers, counsellors, mental health professionals, post-adoption
support organisations, and other adoptive parents. It is also imperative
to acknowledge your own feelings about being an adoptive parent and
to remember that, as adoptive parents, we may not have begun our
relationship with our children with immediate "love". We may have felt
sympathy and care for the child, initially, but in some cases, true love – the
ability to love the child when the child pushes rejection right at you – may
take years to develop.

HELPFUL RESOURCES

Training and information for parents

Adoption and Attachment – A one-year, part-time training course for social workers, therapists, foster carers and adoptive parents. For more information contact Family Futures (see Appendix 2).

Enhancing Adoptive Parenting: A parenting manual for use with new adopters of challenging children by Alan Rushton and Helen Upright, BAAF, forthcoming 2012
This parenting manual is written for adoption support workers and intended to make practical and relevant advice available to the many struggling adopters. The programme aims to support the stability of the adoptive placement, to reduce the level of child problems, and enhance parenting skills and understanding, and improve relationships.

Finding a Way Through: Therapeutic caring for children (DVD), Kate Cairns in conversation with John Simmonds. Shows foster carers and adoptive parents ways of reaching out to damaged children. Available for £35.25 from BAAF (see Appendix 2).

The Impact of Trauma on Children and How Foster Families and Adoptive Families Can Help Them A videotape presentation by Dan Hughes, a psychologist who specialises in helping fostered and adopted children. Dr Hughes discusses how parents can help children develop positive attachments and presents strategies for coping with oppositional behaviour. Available for £100 from Family Futures (see Appendix 2).

It's a Piece of Cake? A parent support programme developed by adopters for adopters Provided by Adoption UK through local authorities. This eight-module course is designed specifically to help adoptive parents gain insight into their children and to help them in their challenging role with their children. Contact Adoption UK for more information (see Appendix 2).

Managing Difficult Behaviour by Clare Pallett *et al* with Eileen Fursland, BAAF, 2008. A unique handbook that provides foster carers and adopters with new skills to help them improve a child's behaviour. Full of useful tips, case examples and exercises.

Remember, also, that many adoptive parents don't have the benefit of a gestation period or a "bonding time" with a young infant. Parents of children adopted after the age of 2½–3 years are presented with a walking, talking individual with his or her own personality, and with the complex effects of early neglect and/or trauma. Consequently, it will take

HELPFUL BOOKS

Related by Adoption: A handbook for grandparents and other relatives by Hedi Argent, BAAF, 2nd edn., 2011. This is a very useful short book on adoption written for family members on the useful role which they can play.

time for you to develop a deep bond with your child, just as your child will take time to attach to you.

'Let me explain about adoption…'

A while after having a child placed, many parents develop an understanding of their child and learn how to respond to their child's various behaviours. However, problems often arise when trying to help the "outside" world understand their children and their children's needs. Daily life may then become a series of stressful events, when activities, such as dealing with schools, grandparents, even those after-school swimming lessons, become difficult because the people involved don't understand your child's behaviours. You may hesitate to discuss adoption with these people, because you don't want to appear to make "excuses" for your child's behaviour. Often, however, open communication is the best policy. The general public usually is unaware of the effects of early trauma on children. Explaining these effects and "educating" others in how best to respond to your child will not only help your child now, but will also help others respond more positively to your child in the future.

A question of guilt and anger

Parenting a child who has attachment difficulties is tough. At times, your anger and frustration with the child may exceed levels you never thought existed within you. You may then begin to question your abilities as a parent, feel guilty about your own anger and reactions to your child, and may feel inadequate to the task of parenting an adopted child. These feelings can be reinforced when other well-meaning people around us (grandparents, friends, social workers, spouses) do not see or understand the child's behaviours. 'Why are you so "uptight"?', they wonder. 'Why are you so strict with your child?' They don't understand your emotions, because they don't spend the same amount of time with the child as you do and they don't see that your child may have rejecting behaviours that are targeted at you – the main caregiver. These will be times of extreme frustration and anxiety for you. It will be important for you to seek the support of the post-adoption organisations and services available to you.

HELPFUL ORGANISATIONS

General organisations that provide help for parents

Increasingly, local authority and voluntary agencies have post-adoption specialists dedicated to providing services for adoptive families. It is worth checking what is available from the agency from whose care your child was adopted, the agency that prepared you to adopt, the local authority where you now live, and any consortia or specialist agencies. Below are several organisations that can provide such support.

Adoption UK

Adoption UK is a parent-to-parent network of over 3,500 established and potential adoptive families. It welcomes enquiries from prospective adopters, offers local support groups across the UK, publishes a range of useful leaflets and a monthly magazine written by and for adopters. It has an online message board facility for members.
Linden House, 55 The Green
South Bar Street
Banbury OX16 9AB
Tel: 01295 752240
Email: admin@adoptionuk.org.uk
www.adoptionuk.org.uk

Family Futures Consortium

Provides an assessment service and an intensive attachment programme. Provides seminars and training for parents, carers and social workers.
3 & 4 Floral Place
7–9 Northampton Grove
London N1 2PL
Tel: 020 7354 4161
Email: contact@familyfutures.co.uk
www.familyfutures.co.uk

Family and Parenting Institute

An independent charity set up to enhance the value and quality of family life. Works to support parents in bringing up children, to promote the well-being of families, and to make society more family friendly. Organises an annual Parents' Week, to celebrate families and parents. Provides 'Pals for Parents' service, a parents' befriending programme.
430 Highgate Studios
53–79 Highgate Road
London NW5 1TL
Tel: 020 7424 3460
Email: info@nfpi.org
www.familyandparenting.org.uk

Fostering Network

Offers advice and information and also has a series of leaflets available on fostering. Also publishes the quarterly magazine *Foster Care*.
87 Blackfriars Road
London SE1 8HA
Tel: 020 7620 6400
www.fostering.net

New Family Social

New Family Social is the UK charity for lesbian, gay, bisexual and transgender adopters, foster carers and their children. NFS provides opportunities to get advice and encouragement to help you get started on your journey, and is a safe space for parents to share support and for children to gain the confidence of knowing other adopted children with LGBT parents.
Tel: 0843 289 9457
www.newfamilysocial.co.uk

Our Place

A registered charity that provides support for families who foster or adopt. The centre offers workshops for parents and for professionals, activities for children, private consultations for parents, a resource room, and opportunities to meet other adoptive/foster parents. It produces a bi-

monthly bulletin of upcoming activities and workshops. There is no fee or geographical restriction to attend the centre. Families attending must have at least one adopted or foster child living in the home. The centre is open Monday–Friday 10am–6pm, with some evening and weekend sessions.
139 Fishponds Road, Eastville
Bristol BS5 6PR
Tel: 0117 951 2433
Email: ourplace1@btconnect.com

Parentline (part of Family Lives)
A confidential helpline that provides information and emotional support to parents.
Tel: Helpline 0808 800 2222
Textphone: 0800 783 6783
www.familylives.org.uk

Positive Parenting Publications and Programmes
Provides information, resources and training for parents and those who support them.
109 Court Oak Road
Birmingham B17 9AA
Tel: 0845 643 1939
www.parenting.org.uk

YoungMinds Parents' Information Service
A telephone service provided by YoungMinds (see Section 4) that gives information and advice for anyone with concerns about the mental health of a child or young person.
Tel: 0808 802 5544
www.youngminds.org.uk/pis

Looking to the future, but acknowledging the past

The fact that your child is adopted and that he or she has had experiences not shared with you, is something you can never change. Often, adoptive parents may feel reluctant to talk with their child about the past. You may even feel uncomfortable being open about your child's adoption with those around you. Especially in the first few months after the child is placed with you, it is tempting to try to forget the child's past entirely in order to focus on your future with your child.

However, in keeping your child's needs at the centre of your thinking, it is important to be aware of signals from your child that he or she needs to talk about and affirm his or her past. The details you choose to discuss with your child and the time of these discussions depends solely upon your child's age and ability to understand certain concepts. After your child has been with you for some time and your attachment deepens, it will become easier to discuss the past. As you focus on your child's needs, you will soon find the right balance of acknowledging, in a healthy way, the facts of your child's adoption and past history. And, as your child's attachment to you becomes more secure, you will become more comfortable with the issue of contact with birth family members.

In short, it's important to live life "normally", while becoming aware of how your child expresses his or her need to affirm the past. "Drip feed" information to your child, bit by bit – you'll soon become familiar with signs that your child needs to talk about the past.

HELPFUL BOOKS

Talking about Adoption to your Adopted Child by Marjorie Morrison, BAAF, 2007
A useful guide that explains how and when to explain to your child that he or she is adopted.

Adoption Conversations: What, when and how to tell by Renée Wolfs, BAAF, 2008
Explores the questions adopted children are likely to ask, with suggestions for helpful explanations and age-appropriate answers.

More Adoption Conversations: What, when and how to tell by Renée Wolfs, BAAF, 2010
Explores the problems that adopted teenagers are likely to confront and provides suggestions for helpful solutions and achievable communication methods.

Give your child small portions of information at opportune moments – often, the casual moments are the most effective – in the car, on the way home from school, for example. It doesn't have to be a long, "prepared" discussion. Just affirming the past in a matter-of-fact way will help your child to incorporate his or her story into their life, and develop a healthy self-image and sense of self.

GOVERNMENT GUIDANCE ABOUT POST-ADOPTION SUPPORT

The Adoption Support Services Regulations 2005, the Adoption Guidance 2011, the National Minimum Standards 2011 and the Practice Guidance on Assessing the Support Needs of Adoptive Families all address support issues.

Adoption Guidance states that:

'The provision of a range of adoption support services is a crucial element of the statutory framework introduced by the [Adoption and Children] Act [2002]. This is based on the recognition that adoptive children and their families are likely to have a range of additional needs.' Guidance 9.1.

Children and adults affected by adoption receive an assessment of their adoption support needs. Service users confirm that the adoption support service provided met or are meeting their assessed needs. When deciding whether to provide a service, or which service to provide, the agency has regard to the assessed needs for adoption support services, listens to the service user's wishes and feelings and considers their welfare and safety. NMS 15.

What can we do if we have trouble handling our child's behaviour?

You could begin by visiting your GP and requesting referral to a consultant child psychologist, psychiatrist or psychotherapist. You could also consult the organisations and services listed in Section 4 as well as those in this section. In addition, local authorities and voluntary adoption agencies provide post-adoption support, but services available from different agencies are variable. Contact your agency to find out what they offer.

Will we be able to have adoption support services from a local authority, even if we adopted several years ago?

Yes. This is described in Section 4. You have a right to an assessment of your adoption support needs. Remember that approaching professionals at a post-adoption/adoption support centre, or adoption or adoption support workers (ASSAs) in your local authority will be important, especially at times of crises, as these professionals will have a good understanding of adoption and therefore could be particularly helpful.

About disruption

"Disruption" is a term commonly used by social workers to describe an adoption (or foster placement) that does not work out.

A placement can disrupt (i.e. break down) for many reasons: for instance, if the child and adoptive parents are unable to bond or attach to each other; if the child has difficulties for which the adoptive parents were not adequately prepared; or if there is not adequate adoption support for the family.

Needless to say, disrupted adoptions bring immense grief, guilt and anger to both the adoptive parents and for the child. Some local authorities and adoption agencies provide a "disruption meeting". This meeting will include the adopters, all involved social workers, the current carers for the child, possibly the birth parents. It is independently chaired. It considers the adoptive parents' histories up to the match, how the match came to be made and what happened during the placement and how it ended. The aim is to inform ongoing work with and planning for the child and to help everyone involved to reflect on, understand and learn from what happened.

HELPFUL RESOURCES

Adoption support services

There are many well-established post-adoption services that provide a service for adoptive families, adopted people and birth parents whose children were adopted. Many of them offer advice and counselling both in person and also on the telephone or by correspondence. Some of them also organise events and training. These services must be registered with Ofsted.

Your local authority has a duty to offer an adoption support service so you can always contact them to see what is available and they should have an appointed adoption support services adviser. If you need specialist support or advice that they cannot provide, they will be able to refer you to a specialist service that will be able to help. Many voluntary agencies also offer a post-adoption service, although, of course, they don't have a statutory duty to do so as do local authorities.

Below we provide a list of independent post-adoption centres.

After Adoption Network A group formed within Adoption UK to help adoptive parents share information and support. You must be a member of Adoption UK to join the network. As a member, you will be given a list of adoptive families in the network who you may contact through meetings or by telephone. For more information, contact Adoption UK (see Appendix 2).

NORCAP

(Adults affected by adoption)
112 Church Road
Wheatley
Oxfordshire OX33 1LU
Tel: 01865 875 000
www.norcap.org.uk

ENGLAND

After Adoption

A voluntary adoption agency and one of the largest providers of adoption support services in the UK. After Adoption provides support to anyone with a connection to adoption as well as finding families for children currently in the care system. They have offices in various parts of England as well as in Wales. They also run different groups, parenting programmes and have an Actionline (see below).
Head Office
Unit 5, City Gate
5 Blantyre Street
Manchester M15 4JJ
Telephone Actionline: 0800 056 8578
www.afteradoption.org.uk

London

Post Adoption Centre

5 Torriano Mews
Torriano Avenue
London NW5 2RZ
Advice line: 020 284 5879 Monday, Tuesday, Wednesday, Friday 10am–1pm, Thurs. 5.30–7.30pm
www.postadoptioncentre.org.uk

Oxfordshire

Parents and Children Together (PACT)
Specialist consultancy services in post adoption, that emphasises multi-agency co-ordination. The PACT Online Post Adoption Service provides a 24-hour information service via a website, and interactive online advice and counselling services during the weekends and evenings.

7 Southern Court
South Street
Reading RG1 4QS
Tel: 0800 731 1845
Email: info@pactcharity.org
www.pactcharity.org

Post-adoption LINK (run by Barnardo's)
Covering Bedfordshire, Cambridgeshire, Essex, Hertfordshire, Norfolk, Peterborough, and Suffolk
Tel: 01206 362540 (10am–1pm, Mon–Fri)

South West Adoption Network (SWAN)
Covering Bath, North East Somerset, Bristol, Gloucestershire, South Gloucestershire, Swindon.
The Park
Daventry Road
Knowle
Bristol BS4 1QD
Tel: 0117 3730265
Email: admin@swan-adoption.org.uk
www.swan-adoption.org.uk

West Midlands

Adoption Support (formerly West Midlands Post-adoption Service)
Suite A, 6th Floor
Albany House, Hurst Street
Birmingham B5 4BD
Tel: 0121 666 6014
Email: info@adoptionsupport.co.uk
www.adoptionsupport.co.uk

Yorkshire

After Adoption Yorkshire
Hollyshaw House
2 Hollyshaw Lane
Leeds LS15 7BD
Tel: 0113 264 6837
Email: info@afteradoptionyorkshire.org.uk
www.afteradoptionyorkshire.org.uk

WALES

After Adoption
A voluntary adoption agency and one of the largest providers of adoption support services in the UK. After Adoption provides support to anyone with a connection to adoption as well as finding families for children currently in the care system. They have offices throughout Wales. They also run different groups, parenting programmes and have an Actionline (see below).
Telephone Actionline: 0800 056 8578
www.afteradoption.org.uk

SCOTLAND

Birthlink
21 Castle Street
Edinburgh EH2 3DN
Tel: 0131 225 6441
www.birthlink.org.uk

Scottish Adoption Advice Service
16 Sandyford Place
Glasgow G3 7NB
Tel: 0141 339 0772
Email: saas@barnardos.org.uk
www.barnardos.org.uk

Helping yourself and helping your child

No two adoptions are the same. You may meet other adoptive families whose experiences will be different from yours.

Hundreds of children in the UK need adoptive families. These children are in need of families in which they can grow and mature within a loving and secure environment. But adoption certainly is not an "easy" road to travel for these children or for their adoptive parents, and it takes a certain type of parent to make the personal sacrifices required of adopters.

As we stated previously, the purpose of this guide is to help you to help yourself on your journey through adoption. No matter what stage you're at in the process – for example, just considering adoption, waiting to be matched with a child, or seeking post-adoption help many years after your child's placement – there are a rapidly increasing number of services and resources which can help you.

Every week, around 100 children in Britain are legally adopted. New families are formed. The interplay of personalities and complex issues faced by both the child and the adults creates unique and varied experiences for the adoptive family. You can be certain, therefore, that you may meet other adoptive families whose experiences might be similar to yours, but rarely exactly the same. Because no two adoptions are the same, you also may encounter services (for example, school and health services) which have little experience of the problems you face with your adopted child. Increased publicity and media attention about adoption increases the general public's understanding of these issues. Yet, despite such publicity and the increasing focus on post-adoption services, you are likely to encounter a significant lack of knowledge and/or understanding about adoption within the general public.

So, what can you do to help yourself?

Firstly, use this guide to communicate with others: with your child's teachers, doctors, babysitter or childminder, birth family members, your own family members, and any other people your child may interact with frequently. Use the guide to inform them about certain issues and/or to find more specific information about these issues.

Secondly, think laterally and creatively! If you and your child are facing specific problems, be aware that solutions to the problem may not always be obvious or straightforward. And remember that there may be several interacting issues that underline one problem. If, for example, your eight-year-old son still has significant problems with soiling and wetting (even though he has been with you for four years), you may have several "causes" to consider: insecurity, anxiety, physical problems and attachment issues, to name a few. But thinking "laterally", you may also have to consider that your son may never have had any formal toilet training, unlike most toddlers. This is a consideration that, understandably, may never have crossed your mind while you were going through the adoption process four years earlier.

As an adoptive parent, you will be challenged, almost daily, to come up with creative strategies to address your child's needs. Use this guide as a starting point for information, and remember that you may have to tailor some of the information and advice in order to suit your child's particular needs.

Parenting children, in general, is not an easy task. Being an adoptive parent adds its own unique challenges. But, by sharing information in a direct, factual and creative manner, adoptive parents can reduce the stress of unexpected problems, address issues in a calm, practical and informed manner, and look forward to a successful and rewarding experience.

Help us to help you! Because the adoption process and associated services are developing and changing so rapidly, this guide may not provide all the answers you may need. Inevitably, with new government initiatives and rapid growth in post-adoption services, you may come across organisations, publications or services that are not listed here. If so, please inform us.

By sharing information in a direct, factual and creative manner, adoptive parents can reduce the stress of unexpected problems, address issues in a calm, practical and informed manner, and look forward to a successful and rewarding experience for their children and for themselves.

Appendices

Appendix 1:
Books, journals and magazines

Appendix 2:
Organisations, government agencies, websites

Appendix 3:
Extracts from National Minimum Standards for Adoption (2011) applicable to the provision of adoption services

Appendix 4:
The Adopters' Charter

Appendix 1: Books, journals and magazines

The publications listed here are a compilation of most of the publications listed within this handbook, and are only a sample of the information available. See www.baaf.org.uk for more books published by BAAF.

Books for prospective adopters/ adoptive parents

Guides to adoptive parenting

Adopted Children Speaking by Caroline Thomas and Verna Beckford, BAAF, 1999. Provides moving and poignant testimonies which offer revealing insights into children's feelings about adoption.

Adopters on Adoption: Reflections on parenthood and children by David Howe, BAAF, 1996. This absorbing collection of personal stories covers topics including assessment and preparation, feelings towards birth mothers, and biology, infertility, and parenting secure children.

Adopting a Child by Jenifer Lord, BAAF, 2011 (9th edition). This guide describes what adoption means and how to go about it, including procedures and practices, legal requirements and the costs involved.

Adoption Conversations: What, when and how to tell, by Renée Wolfs, BAAF, 2008. Explores the questions adopted children are likely to ask, with suggestions for helpful explanations and age-appropriate answers.

Approaching Fatherhood: A guide for adoptive dads, by Paul May, BAAF, 2005. The first book in the UK to combine adoptive fathers' experiences with a guide to the adoption process, from the man's point of view.

Attachment, Trauma and Resilience, by Kate Cairns, BAAF, 2002. Kate draws on the wealth of her personal and professional experience to offer a vivid glimpse into life with children who have experienced attachment difficulties, abuse and trauma, and shows in a range of everyday situations how her family responded.

Checklist for Prospective Adopters Available from Adoption UK. Lists questions prospective adopters should consider and should discuss with their social worker at all stages of the adoption process.

Child Adoption: A guidebook for adoptive parents and their advisors by Rene Hoksbergen, Jessica Kingsley Publishers, 1997. A comprehensive guide written by the general director of the Adoption Centre at Utrecht University. Discusses many issues, including preparing for adoption, adopting children from different ethnic and cultural backgrounds, and helping the child adjust to school.

Could you be my Parent? edited by Leonie Sturge-Moore, BAAF, 2005. This enthralling anthology gathers together a selection of informative, often moving articles and interviews from Be My Parent, BAAF's family-finding newspaper to create a fascinating snapshot of the process of adoption and foster care.

The Dynamics of Adoption: Social and personal perspectives edited by Amal Treacher and Ilan Katz, Jessica Kingsley, 2000. A collection of essays about adoption.

First Steps in Parenting the Child Who Hurts: Tiddlers and toddlers by Caroline Archer, Jessica Kingsley, 1999. Discusses the attachment and developmental issues that arise when even the youngest child is in your care.

'Just a member of the family': Families and children who adopt by Bridget Betts, video/ DVD, BAAF, 2005. This is the first film to look at adoption from a child's point of view, featuring a number of birth children who have had the experience of adopting a child into their family. Available on video or DVD.

Lesbian and Gay Fostering and Adoption: Extraordinary, yet ordinary edited by Stephen

Hicks and Janet McDermott, Jessica Kingsley Publishers, 1999. Diverse stories from lesbian and gay adopters and foster carers about caring for young children.

Life Story Work by Tony Ryan and Rodger Walker, BAAF, 2007 (3rd edn). A popular guide that provides insight, ideas and exercises to use for life story work.

Linking and Introductions: Helping children join adoptive families by Sheila Byrne, BAAF, 2001. Provides useful practice guidance on the major stages of linking and introductions.

Looking After our Own: The stories of black and Asian adopters edited by Hope Massiah, BAAF, 2005. An inspiring collection looking at the experiences of nine black and Asian adoptive families and their children.

More Adoption Conversations: What, when and how to tell, by Renée Wolfs, BAAF, 2010. Explores the problems that adopted teenagers are likely to confront and provides suggestions for helpful solutions and achievable communication methods.

Next Steps in Parenting the Child Who Hurts: Tykes and teens by Caroline Archer, Jessica Kingsley, 1999. This book follows on logically from the First Steps book and continues into the challenging journey through childhood and into adolescence.

Novices, Old Hands and Professionals: Adoption by single people by Morag Owen, BAAF, 1999. Documents and comments on the experiences of single adopters and their children.

One of the Family: A handbook for kinship carers by Hedi Argent, BAAF, 2005. This handbook aims to give families and friends who may become kinship carers information about the choices they can make, the assessment process, legal framework and the support they can expect.

The Pink Guide to Adoption for Lesbians and Gay Men by Nicola Hill, BAAF, 2009. An essential step-by-step guide to the adoption process for lesbians and gay men considering adoption,

which also includes interviews with and stories from several lesbians and gay men at various stages of the adoption process.

Preparing to Adopt: A training pack for preparation groups by Eileen Fursland, BAAF, 2006 (2nd edn). A training pack, consisting of a trainer's guide, an applicant's workbook and a video, designed to prepare prospective adopters for all the aspects of the adoption process.

Real Parents, Real Children: Parenting the adopted child by Holly van Gulden and Lisa Bartels-Rabb, Crossroad Publishing, 1993. Takes parents and professionals through the stages of child development, explaining what adopted children at each age commonly think and feel about adoption and how parents can respond.

Related by Adoption: A handbook for grandparents and other relatives by Hedi Argent with a contribution from Kate Cairns, BAAF, 2011 (2nd edition). This brief and sensitively written handbook aims to give grandparents-to-be and other relatives information about adoption today and how the wider family can support building a family through adoption.

Talking about Adoption to your Adopted Child by Marjorie Morrison, BAAF, 2004 (3rd edition). A useful guide that advises how and when to explain to your child that he or she is adopted.

Parenting Matters: A new forthcoming series (2012) of short informative books that aim to offer expert information on topics of interest, focusing on health-related conditions. Look out for these on www.baaf.org.uk.

Legal and financial issues

Adoption Now: Law, regulations, guidance and standards by Fergus Smith and Roy Stewart with Alexandra Conroy Harris, BAAF, 2011 (2nd edition). A handy spiral-bound pocket book, covering all essential information on the law, regulations, guidance and standards relating to adoption today.

Child Care Law: A summary of the law in England and Wales by Deborah Cullen and Mary Lane, BAAF, 2006. Quick-reference guide to the law (in England and Wales) regarding the care of children.

Child Care Law: Scotland by Alexandra Plumtree, BAAF, 2005. Quick-reference guide to the law (in Scotland) regarding the care of children.

The Children Act and the Courts: A guide for parents Available from the Department of Health. A booklet that describes how the Children Act affects parents and children involved in court cases.

The Children Act and Local Authorities: A guide for parents Available from the Department of Health. A booklet that describes the Children Act, the role of local authorities, and what services and entitlements parents can expect as a result of the Act.

Effective Panels (4th edn) by Jenifer Lord and Deborah Cullen, BAAF, forthcoming 2012. Provides guidance on regulations, process and good practice in adoption and permanence panels.

Special Education Handbook: The law on children with special needs Available from the Advisory Centre for Education. Explains the process of obtaining a statement of special educational needs and various aspects of the statementing process. See Appendix 2 for contact details.

Schooling

Attachment, Developmental Trauma and Executive Functioning Difficulties in the School Setting, by Marion Allen, Family Futures, 2008. Provides strategies and interventions to manage behaviour and establish an environment which will enable children to achieve their personal and academic potential.

Attachment in the Classroom: The links between children's early experience, emotional wellbeing and performance in school, by Heather Geddes, Worth Publishing, 2006. Explores the significance of the relationship between the pupil, the teacher and the learning task, linking it to emotional development, behaviour and attachment experiences.

Banished to the Exclusion Zone: School exclusion and the law Available from the Coram Children's Legal Centre. See Appendix 2 for contact details.

Inside I'm Hurting: Practical strategies for supporting children with attachment difficulties in schools, by Louise Michelle Bombèr, Worth Publishing, 2007. Provides educational professionals with a much needed classroom handbook of strategies, practical tools and the confidence for supporting children (who have experienced trauma) from an attachment perspective.

Learn the Child: Helping looked after children to learn by Kate Cairns and Chris Stanway, BAAF, 2004. A resource pack, consisting of a book and CD ROM, which looks at the long-term effects of trauma in childhood and how this can affect learning, with suggestions for how traumatised children can best be supported by carers and professionals.

Mental Health in Your School: A guide for teachers and others working in schools by Peter Wilson, YoungMinds, 1996, available from Jessica Kingsley (see below). A practical and helpful guidebook.

Nobody Ever Told Us School Mattered: Raising the educational attainments of children in care edited by Sonia Jackson, BAAF, 2001. An anthology that considers what can be done to ensure that looked after children have a better chance to succeed.

Promoting Children's Mental Health within Early Years and School Settings Department for Education and Skills (DfES), 2001. Provides examples of mental health initiatives taking place in schools and gives advice on helping children who have mental health problems or who have difficulties at school.

Special Educational Needs: A guide for parents Department for Education and Skills (DfES). See Appendix 2 for contact details.

Special Needs: A guide for parents and carers of Jewish children with special educational needs Available from the Board of Deputies of British Jews, Tel: 020 7543 5400.

Stop Wasting my Time! Case studies of pupils with attachment issues in schools with special reference to looked after and adopted children, by Eileen Bebbington, Post Adoption Central Support. A helpful booklet which will help teachers understand attachment issues and create a calmer learning situation.

Supporting Children in Public Care in Schools: A resource for trainers of teachers, carers and social workers, by John Holland and Catherine Randerson, Jessica Kingsley Publishers, 2005. A comprehensive training resource which provides guidance on how to support children who have faced loss as a result of significant changes in placement.

Physical and mental health and disability issues

Child and Adolescent Mental Health Services: Everybody's business National Assembly for Wales. Available from 029 2082 3480 or www.wales.gov.uk

Every Child is Special: Placing disabled children for permanence by Jennifer Cousins, BAAF, 2006. Contains useful information for social workers, carers and parents about family placement of children with severe to profound disabilities.

Learning Disabilities in Children by Peter Burke and Katy Cigno, Blackwell Science, 2000. Explains how learning difficulties are defined and examines their impact on family life. The book is aimed at those working in child welfare, social work and community care.

The Mental Health Needs of Looked After Children edited by Joanna Richardson and Carol Joughin, Gaskell, 2000. Describes mental health problems of children in care. Written primarily for social workers and foster carers, this book emphasises the importance of prevention and early recognition of mental health problems.

Parent Participation: Improving services for disabled children, Council for Disabled Children and Contact a Family

Parents as Partners in the Treatment of Dissociative Children by Frances S. Waters, MSW, in The Dissociative Child: Diagnosis, Treatment and Management by J. Silberg, 1996, The Sidran Press. Text available on www.sidran.org/side13.html

The Patient's Charter: Services for children and young people produced by the Department of Health. Outlines the rights and standards for children's care within the NHS. (Note: Although still applicable to Wales and Scotland, in England the Patient's Charter was replaced by the Government's Health Plan for 2001.)

Whatever Happened to Adam? by Hedi Argent, BAAF, 1996. Tells the stories of disabled people who were adopted or fostered.

Attachment issues

Attachment Handbook for Foster Care and Adoption by Gillian Schofield and Mary Beek, BAAF, 2006. A comprehensive and authoritative textbook which provides an accessible account of core attachment concepts.

Attachment Theory, Child Maltreatment and Family Support by David Howe et al, Macmillan, 1999. Offers a comprehensive account of how social developmental perspectives and attachment theory can illuminate practice in the field of child protection and family support, drawing extensively on case study material.

Attachment, Trauma and Healing: Understanding and treating attachment disorder in children and families by Terry M. Levy and Michael Orlans, Child Welfare League of America Press, 1998, USA. Provides a detailed, but more clinically based approach to attachment issues in children.

Attachment, Trauma and Resilience by Kate Cairns, BAAF, 2002. Kate, her husband and three birth children have fostered 12 children. She draws on the wealth of her personal and professional experience to offer a vivid glimpse into life with children who have experienced attachment difficulties, abuse and trauma.

Building the Bonds of Attachment by Daniel Hughes, Jason Aronson, 2006. Critically acclaimed book for those who strive to assist poorly attached children, which blends attachment theory, research, and trauma theory with general principles of parenting and family therapy.

Connecting with Kids through Stories: Using narratives to facilitate attachment in adopted children, by Denise Lacher, Todd Nichols and Joanne May, Jessica Kingsley Publishers, 2005. An accessible guide to family attachment narrative therapy for the parents of adopted or fostered children.

Facilitating Developmental Attachment: The road to emotional recovery and behavioral change in foster and adopted children by Daniel A. Hughes, Jason Aronson, Inc., 1997, USA. An easy-to-read book written by a leading clinical psychologist in the U.S. who specialises in helping foster and adopted children and families. The book provides an in-depth look at attachment issues in children and provides many strategies for parents.

Finding a Way Through: Therapeutic caring for children, Kate Cairns in conversation with John Simmonds, video, BAAF, 2003. An inspirational and powerful video in which John Simmonds talks to Kate Cairns, author of Attachment, Trauma and Resilience, about being a parent/

carer and how parents can help traumatised children to heal.

Fostering Attachments: Long-term outcomes in family group care, by Brian Cairns, BAAF, 2004. Brian, who, along with Kate Cairns and their three birth children, fostered 12 children, takes a less theoretical view to examine the process of parenting traumatised children and the benefits of family group membership in aiding learning and recovery.

Together in Time, by Ruth and Ed Royce, BAAF, 2008. Ruth and Ed look back on their decision to adopt a boy with attachment difficulties, the fear that their family was falling apart, and their experience of music and art therapy.

Trauma, Attachment and Family Permanence: Fear can stop you loving, edited by Caroline Archer and Alan Burnell, Jessica Kingsley Publishers, 2003. Draws on the programmes offered by Family Futures to explore the challenges faced by the professional or parent who seeks to promote family permanence. Brings together a rich selection of ideas.

Understanding Attachment and Attachment Disorders: Theory, evidence and practice by Vivien Prior and Danya Glaser, Jessica Kingsley Publishers, 2006. An examination and discussion of the scientific evidence on attachment, its influence on development, and attachment disorders.

Intercountry adoption

Children Adopted from Abroad: Key health and developmental issues, BAAF, 2004. A pamphlet aimed at intercountry adopters, which explains and advises on possible child health problems and the screening of children adopted from overseas.

Intercountry Adoption by Cherry Harnott, BAAF, 2006. A pamphlet which describes the intercountry adoption process, issues and implications for families involved, and basic practical guidance on procedures and rules.

Intercountry Adoption: Developments, trends and perspectives edited by Peter Selman, BAAF, 2000. An anthology about several aspects of intercountry adoption as seen from diverse perspectives – parents, young people, researchers and practitioners.

A Procedural Guide to Intercountry Adoption Available from the Intercountry Adoption Centre. See Appendix 2 for contact details.

Policy and Practice Implications from the English and Romanian Adoptees (ERA) Study: Forty-five key questions by Michael Rutter *et al*, BAAF, 2009. Focuses on the policy and practice implications of this internationally known study, which answers 45 key questions most often posed by practitioners and policy makers.

Search and reunion

Adoption, Search and Reunion by David Howe and Julia Feast, BAAF, 2003. An investigation into why some adopted adults search for their birth parents, while others do not. Centres on the long-term experiences of 500 adults who were placed for adoption as children. See Appendix 2 for contact details.

Searching Questions: Identity, origins and adoption by Julia Feast and Terry Philpot, BAAF, 2003 (book and video). Highlights the issues involved in searching and reunion. Designed for training, discussion groups or individuals who have been affected by these subjects.

Other books/articles

'Adoption after bereavement' by Eve Hopkirk, *Adoption & Fostering*, 26:1, BAAF, 2002.

'Adoption with contact: a study of adoptive parents and the impact of continuing contact with families of origin' by M. Sykes, *Adoption & Fostering*, 24:2, BAAF, 2000.

A Child's Journey through Placement by Vera Fahlberg, BAAF, 1994. Clear, informative and insightful and full of practical ideas and case examples, this essential reference book contains the knowledge base and skills for understanding and working with children and their families.

Children Exposed to Parental Substance Misuse edited by Rena Phillips, BAAF, 2004. This anthology looks at the effects on children of drugs, alcohol and other substances misused by parents, especially mothers, during pregnancy. Contains invaluable tools, suggestions and resources.

The Colours in Me: Writing and poetry by adopted children and young people edited by Perlita Harris, BAAF, 2008. Over 80 contributors, ranging from four to 20 years of age, tell it like it is, revealing what it feels like and what it means to be adopted.

Coming Home to Self: Healing the primal wound by Nancy Newton Verrier, BAAF, 2010. The sequel to *The Primal Wound*, this book examines the effects of separation trauma on brain development and looks at ways of regulating emotions and healing the self.

Do You Know Someone Who Has Been Sexually Abused? Available from YoungMinds. Produced specifically for parents. See Appendix 2 for contact details.

'Early adversity and adoptive solutions' by Ann and Alan Clarke, in *Adoption & Fostering*, 25:1, BAAF, 2001.

'Family building in adoption' by B. Prynn, *Adoption & Fostering*, 25:1, 2001.

I Wish I had been Born from You: Poems and reflections on adoption, by Karen Lomas, BAAF, 2009. Written by a mother, with contributions from her adopted daughter, this honest and heartfelt collection charts a moving and emotional adoption journey of getting to know one another and becoming a family.

In Search of Belonging: Reflections of transracially adopted children edited by Perlita Harris, BAAF, 2006. This is the first UK publication to give voice to child and adult transracial adoptees, bringing together poetry, artwork, memoirs and writings from over 50 transracial and transnational UK adoptees.

Mother Me: An adopted woman's journey to motherhood by Zara H Phillips, BAAF, 2008. This frank and honest account explores the far-reaching impact of adoption on the author's childhood, adolescence, relationships and self-esteem, along with a unique insight into pregnancy and motherhood from the perspective of an adopted woman.

The Primal Wound: Understanding the adopted child by Nancy Newton Verrier, BAAF, 2009. A classic in adoption literature, in this book the author explores what she calls the "primal wound" that results when a child is separated from his or her mother, and the trauma and life-long consequences that can result.

Siblings in Late Permanent Placements by Alan Rushton et al, BAAF, 2001. A research study that explores the complexities of sibling placements.

Special and Odd by James Mulholland, BAAF, 2007. A revealing and extraordinarily witty memoir in which the author tells the story of how he met his birth mother, 29 years after being given up for adoption, and the effect this had on him and his adoptive family.

Together or Apart? Assessing brothers and sisters for permanent placement by Jenifer Lord and Sarah Borthwick, BAAF, 2008 (2nd edn). Looks at the factors that should be considered in placing sibling groups.

We Are Family: Sibling relationships in placement and beyond edited by Audrey Mullender, BAAF, 1999. An anthology on various aspects of sibling relationships from diverse perspectives.

Books for children who have been adopted

Adoption: What it is and what it means by Shaila Shah, BAAF, 2003. A short, brightly illustrated guide to adoption for children and young people, which sets out information about the processes and procedures simply and clearly.

Chester and Daisy Move On by Angela Lidster, illustrations by Robyn Allpress, BAAF, 1995. This engaging picture book is for use with children who are moving on to adoption. It tells the story of Chester and Daisy, two little bear cubs who have to leave their parents and live with a new bear family.

Children's Book Series by Sheila Byrne and Leigh Chambers, illustrations by Sarah Rawlings, BAAF. When children are separated from their birth families, part of their very self is in jeopardy. They need help to make sense of their experiences and individual history. This unique series of popular books for use with separated children is designed to do just that.

Titles include:

Joining together – Jo's story A story about a step-parent adoption.

Feeling safe – Tina's story A story about a girl who has to go into foster care following abuse in the home.

Living with a new family – Nadia and Rashid's story A story about a brother and sister being adopted.

Belonging doesn't mean forgetting – Nathan's story A story about a four-year-old boy being adopted.

Hoping for the best – Jack's story A story about an adoption that did not work out.

Dad David, Baba Chris and Me by Ed Merchant, BAAF, 2010. This brightly illustrated book for children aged 5–10 years old tells the story of Ben's life with his adoptive gay parents and how, after teasing at school, his teacher helps the class to understand that children live in all kinds of families.

Draw on Your Emotions: Creative ways to explore, express and understand important feelings by Margot Sunderland and Philip Engleheart, Speechmark Publishing Ltd., 1993. A series of structured, easy picture exercises to help people of all ages express, communicate and deal more effectively with their emotions in

everyday life. Designed for health professionals, but can be used by parents with their children.
Tel: 01304 226900
email: orders@smallwood.co.uk

Josh and Jaz have Three Mums by Hedi Argent, BAAF, 2007. This brightly illustrated book tells the story of Josh and Jaz, five-year-old twins who have been adopted by a lesbian couple. Having to draw a family tree for school teaches their class about different family structures and diversity.

Life Story Work: What it is and what it means by Shaila Shah and Hedi Argent, BAAF, 2006. This new booklet, for children and young people who are embarking on life story work or are already doing it, explains what it is and how it is undertaken.

My Life and Me by Jean Camis, BAAF, 2001. A colourful and comprehensive life story workbook which will help children develop and record memories and recollections of their past and their birth family. With comprehensive guidelines for the adult working with the child.

The Most Precious Present in the World by Becky Edwards, BAAF, 2009. Taking the form of a dialogue between a little girl, Mia, and her adoptive mother, this book explores questions that might preoccupy an adopted child, including why she looks different to her adoptive parents and why her birth mother didn't want to keep her.

The Nutmeg series by Judith Foxon, illustrated by Sarah Rawlings, BAAF.

Nutmeg Gets Adopted 2001

Nutmeg Gets Cross 2002

Nutmeg Gets a Letter 2003

Nutmeg Gets a Little Help 2004

Nutmeg Gets into Trouble 2006

Nutmeg Gets a Little Sister 2007

A colourful storybook series telling the story of Nutmeg the squirrel and his brother and sister, who go to live with a new family after their birth

mother realises she cannot keep them safe. The books cover the painful feelings that are likely to surface following adoption; contact; post-adoption support work; and the adopted child in education.

Oh Brother! Tom gets a new adopted brother by Claire Friday, Adoption UK, 2005. Aimed at children aged between 7–11 years, this book tells the story of Tom, a birth child, whose parents decide to adopt another child, looking at Tom's hopes, fears and expectations through the approval and matching process and once Billy joins the family.

Stories for Troubled Children by Margot Sunderland, Speechmark Publishing. Five books to help children think about their feelings and to work through issues that trouble them.

Willy and the Wobbly House a story for children who are anxious or obsessional;

A Wibble Called Biley (and a Few Honks) a story for children who have hardened their hearts or who have become bullies;

A Pea Called Mildred to help children pursue their hopes and dreams;

A Nifflenoo Called Nevermind for children who bottle up their feelings;

The Frog Who Longed for the Moon to Smile for children who yearn for someone they love.

The Teazles' Baby Bunny by Susan Bagnall, BAAF, 2008. A colourful picture book for young children aged two to four years which tells the simple story of the Teazle rabbits and their adoption of a baby bunny.

What Happens in Court? by Hedi Argent and Mary Lane, BAAF, 2003. A user-friendly guide for adopted and fostered children which will help them understand the role that a court might play in their lives.

What is Contact? by Hedi Argent, BAAF, 2004. A colourful children's guide which describes what contact or "keeping in touch" means for children who are not living with their birth family.

What is a Disability? by Hedi Argent, BAAF, 2004. This children's guide explains what disabilities are and what they can mean for those who have them, with the understanding that every child is special and children with disabilities are more special in a different way.

Where is Poppy's Panda? by David Pitcher, BAAF, 2009. This beautifully illustrated book for children aged three and above explores transition, loss and change and the importance of maintaining continuity in a child's life.

Journals and magazines

Adoption & Fostering Quarterly journal of BAAF. Presents current issues in practice, policy, law and research in foster care and adoption throughout the UK. For anyone involved in foster care and adoption. Available by subscription from BAAF (see Appendix 2).

Adoption Today Monthly magazine of Adoption UK. Directed mainly at people who have adopted or who are considering adoption. Part I of the magazine includes articles, news items, letters and book reviews about adoption. Part II of the magazine, **Children Who Wait**; also available online at www.adoptionuk.org.uk, provides information about children currently waiting to be adopted. The magazine is free with membership in Adoption UK (see Appendix 2).

Be My Parent Monthly UK-wide family-finding newspaper published by BAAF. Subscribers to Be My Parent include approved adopters, those waiting to be approved and those who have only just begun to think about adopting or permanently fostering. Children of all ages and with a wide range of needs from all over the country are featured each month. Available by subscription from BAAF (see Appendix 2). Also available online at www.bemyparent.org.uk.

Appendix 2: Organisations, government agencies, websites

The following list details some key organisations that could be useful. They have been checked at the time of going to press, but details can change! It's best to search online as there is a wealth of information available on the internet, although you must be careful to select those organisations which are authoritative sources.

ADDISS
(The National Attention Deficit Disorder Information and Support Service)

Provides information and resources about ADHD for parents, teachers and health professionals. In addition to publications, ADDISS resources include conferences, training and local support groups.

112 Station Road
Edgware
Middlesex HA8 7BJ
Tel: 020 8952 2800
email: info@addiss.co.uk
www.addiss.co.uk

ADD/ADHD Family Support Group UK

209–211 City Road
London EC1V 1JN
Helpline: 0808 808 3555
email: info@cafamily.org.uk
www.cafamily.org.uk

ADHD UK Alliance

Publishes the newsletter, 'ADDvance'. Membership is free for parents and support groups.

Enquire at:
209–211 City Road
London EC1V 1JN
Tel: 020 7608 8760
email: info@adhdalliance.org.uk

Adoption agencies

Please refer to: *Adopting a Child*, available from BAAF. This best-selling guide is regularly updated and has a list of adoption agencies throughout the UK.

Adoption Contact Register for England and Wales

The General Register Office
Adoption Section
Smedley Hydro, Trafalgar Road
Southport, Merseyside PR8 2HH
Tel: 0845 603 7788
www.direct.gov.uk

Adoption Contact Register Office for Scotland

C/o Birthlink
21 Castle Street
Edinburgh EH2 3DN
Tel: 0131 225 6441
www.birthlink.org.uk

Adoption Register for England and Wales

Unit 4, Pavilion Business Park
Royds Hall Road, Wortley
Leeds LS12 6AJ
Tel: 0845 450 3931
email: mail@adoptionregister.org.uk
www.adoptionregister.org.uk

Adoption Register for Scotland

113 Rose Street
Edinburgh EH2 3DT
Tel: 0131 226 9279
email: sar@scotlandsadoptionregister.org.uk
www.scotlandsadoptionregister.org.uk

Adoption UK

A UK-wide self-help group run by adoptive parents who offer support before, during and after adoption. Services include a helpline; a magazine that includes details of children waiting for adoption; messageboards for adopters and prospective adopters to share knowledge and support each other; and a variety of printed information about all aspects of adoption.

Linden House
55 The Green
South Bar Street
Banbury
Oxfordshire OX16 9AB
Tel: 01295 752240
www.adoptionuk.org.uk

Adoptive Parents Association of Ireland

Glendalough Post Office
County Wicklow, Ireland
Tel: 00 35 3404 45184
email: apai@tinet.ie

Advisory Centre for Education (ACE)

Provides information about all aspects of state education and helps parents who are dealing with schools or education authorities.
Unit 1C, Aberdeen Studios
22 Highbury Grove, London N5 2DQ
General advice line: 0808 800 5793
"Exclusion" advice line: 0808 800 0327
www.ace-ed.org.uk

After Adoption

Offers a wide range of services and provides information, support and advice to all those affected by adoption.
Head Office
Unit 5
Citygate
5 Blantyre Street
Manchester M15 4JJ
Tel: 0800 0568 578 (for service users)
0161 839 493 (for professionals)
www.afteradoption.org.uk

Anna Freud Centre

A research and treatment centre for children and young people who have a range of emotional, behavioural and developmental difficulties. Information about its services, as well as summaries of research into attachment and other emotional/behavioural difficulties are provided on its website.
12 Maresfield Gardens
London NW3 5SU
Tel: 020 7794 2313
email: info@annafreud.org
www.annafreudcentre.org

Association for Child and Adolescent Mental Health

An association for professionals of various disciplines who are involved with children. It arranges seminars and publishes professional journals. It does not provide an advice service.

39–41 Union Street, London SE1 1SD
Tel: 020 7403 7458
email: ingrid.king@acamh.org.uk
www.acamh.org.uk

Association of Child Psychotherapists (ACP)

Maintains register of accredited child psychotherapists and gives details of local child psychotherapists.

120 West Heath Road
London NW3 7TU
Tel: 020 8458 1609
email: inquiries@acp.uk.net
www.childpsychotherapy.org.uk

Benefit Enquiry Line

Tel: 0800 882 200
Textphone: 0800 243355
Email: BEL-customer-services@DWP.gsi.gov.uk
www.direct.gov.uk/disability-money

Birthlink (formerly Family Care Birthlink)

Offers post-adoption counselling and runs Scotland's only contact register.

21 Castle Street
Edinburgh EH2 3DN
Tel: 0131 225 6441
email: mail@birthlink.org.uk
www.birthlink.org.uk

British Association for Adoption and Fostering (BAAF)

UK-wide membership organisation for agencies and individuals concerned with adoption and fostering. Provides publications for adopters, social work practitioners and other professionals, and a family-finding service, *Be My Parent*. Also provides information and advice, and organises conferences and seminars. Offices in England, Scotland, Wales and Northern Ireland.

Head Office
Saffron House, 6–10 Kirby Street
London EC1N 8TS
Tel: 020 7421 2600
www.baaf.org.uk

British Association for Counselling and Psychotherapy (BACP)

Send SAE for details of local counsellors and psychotherapists.

BACP House
15 St John's Business Park
Lutterworth
LE17 4HB
Tel: 01445 883300
Monday–Friday 9.30am–3pm (information)
email: enquiries@bacp.co.uk
www.bacp.co.uk

The British Association of Psychotherapists (BAP)

The training and professional institution of psychoanalytic psychotherapists, analytical psycholoists (Jungian) and child psychotherapists.
37 Mapesbury Road
London NW2 4HJ
Tel: 020 8452 9823
email: mail@bap-psychotherapy.org
www.bap-psychotherapy.org

British Institute for Learning Disabilities (BILD)

Services include information about various learning disabilities, resources, conferences and events. Also supports research into learning disabilities.

Campion House, Green Street
Kidderminster, Worcestershire DY10 1JL
Tel: 01562 723 010
email: enquiries@bild.org.uk
www.bild.org.uk

Caspari Foundation (formerly Forum for Educational Therapy and Therapeutic Teaching, FAETT)

Dedicated to promoting educational therapy and therapeutic learning to help children who have emotional barriers that can impair learning. Organises lectures and events.

55 Eagle Wharf Road
London N1 7ER
Tel: 020 7704 1977
email: admin@caspari.org.uk
www.caspari.org.uk

The Centre for Child Mental Health

Promotes awareness of the emotional well-being and mental health of children. Disseminates research to health professionals, parents and the media through conferences, publications and workshops.

2–18 Britannia Row
London N1 8PA
Tel: 020 7354 2913
email: info@childmentalhealthcentre.org
www.childmentalhealthcentre.org

Children and Families Across Borders (CFAB)

A voluntary organisation that helps families and individuals whose lives are split between different countries.

Canterbury Court, Unit 1.03
1–3 Brixton Road, London SW9 6DE
Tel: 020 7735 8941
www.cfab.uk.net

Children and Family Courts Advisory and Support Service (CAFCASS)

CAFCASS looks after the interests of children involved in family proceedings. They work with children and their families and advise the courts on what they consider to be in the best interests of children.

6th Floor, Sanctuary Buildings
Great Smith Street
London SW1P 3BT
Tel: 0844 353 3350
email: webenquiries@cafcass.gov.uk
www.cafcass.gov.uk

Children in Scotland

Provides a national information and advice service, Enquire, for parents, professionals, children and young people who have questions about special educational needs.

Princes House, 5 Shandwick Place
Edinburgh EH2 4RG
Helpline: 0845 123 2303
Tel: 0131 228 8484
email: info@childreninscotland.org.uk
www.childreninscotland.org.uk

The Children's Society

UK-wide charity which provides projects and information for children and families who are experiencing difficulties, including children at risk, disabled children, children affected by adult substance misuse, post-adoption and advocacy services, and more.

Edward Rudolf House, Margery Street
London WC1X 0JL
Tel: 0845 300 1128
email: supporteraction@childrens
society.org.uk
www.childrenssociety.org.uk

Community Legal Service

A government initiative designed to ensure everyone has access to quality legal advice and information. The service can be provided by CABs, solicitors' firms and legal advice centres that have been awarded the Community Legal Service Quality mark. You can find the *Community Legal Service Directory* at your local library and online. It lists all law firms and advice centres that have the Quality Mark, and indicates whether firms offer free advice or if they charge for advice.

Tel: 0845 345 4345 for information about CLS providers or about the CLS directory.
www.legalservices.gov.uk/civil.asp

Contact a Family

Provides information for parents on over 2,000 rare medical conditions, including information about support groups, and publishes a useful directory, 'The CAF Directory of Specific Conditions and Rare Disorders – 2002'. There is also a freephone helpline for parents seeking information regarding help for disabled children.

209–211 City Road, London EC1V 1JN
Helpline: 0808 808 3555
Monday–Friday 10am–4pm
Tel: 020 7608 8700
email: info@cafamily.org.uk
www.cafamily.org.uk

ContinYou
(formerly Special Education Consortium)

Unit C1
Grovelands Court
Grovelands Estate
Longford Road, Exhall
Coventry CV7 9NE
Tel: 024 7658 8440
www.continyou.org.uk

Coram Children's Legal Centre

Specialises in law and policy affecting children and young people. Produces information sheets and booklets. In addition to policy and campaign work, also provides an advice and information service (free and confidential legal advice).

Helpline: 9898 802 0008 (free legal advice)
email: clc@essex.ac.uk
www.coramchildrenslegalcentre.com

Council for Disabled Children

Promotes collaborative work between different organisations providing services and support for children and young people with disabilities and special educational needs. Offers a range of services including consultancy, training, information, publications and conferences.

8 Wakley Street, London EC1V 7QE
Tel: 020 7843 1900
email: cdc@ncb.org.uk
www.ncb.org.uk/cdc

The Court Service

www.justice.gov.uk

Department for Education (DfE)

Provides information for parents about all aspects of education and schools. The DfE website offers a Parents' Centre that provides specific and comprehensive information about SEN. Contact the DfE publications department to find out about specific information for parents, such as the *SEN Guide for Parents*, and for a copy of the *Code of Practice*.

Tel: 0370 000 2288
Fax: 01928 738248
www.education.gov.uk

Department of Health Publications

www.dh.gov.uk/en/publicationsandstatistics/index.htm

Depression Alliance

Promotes greater understanding of depression to reduce the stigma associated with it. Produces a free booklet, 'The Young Person's Guide to Stress'.

20 Great Dover Street
London SE1 4LX
Tel: 0845 123 2320
Email: information:depressionalliance.org
www.depressionalliance.org

DORE (UK) Ltd (formerly Dyslexia, Dyspraxia and Attention Treatment Centre (DDAT))

Provides assessment, consultation and treatment for children, adolescents and adults who may have dyslexia, dyspraxia or attention difficulties. Contact the Centre for further information about its services and its fees.

Bridgeway House
Bridgeways
Stratford upon Avon
CV37 6YY
Tel: 0333 123 0100
email: info@dore.co.uk
www.dore.co.uk

Faith in Families (formerly Catholic Children's Society (Nottingham))

7 Colwick Road, West Bridgford
Nottingham NG2 5FR
Tel: 0115 955 8811
email: enquiries@faithinfamilies.org
www.faithinfamilies.org

Family and Parenting Institute

Supports parents and offers practical help in bringing up children and promotes the well-being of families. Services include publications and conferences.

430 Highgate Studios
53–79 Highgate Road
London NW5 1TL
Tel: 020 7424 3460
email: info@familyandparenting.org
www.familyandparenting.org

Family Futures Consortium Ltd

An adoption and adoption support agency, which specialises in therapeutic work for children who have experienced early trauma and who have attachment difficulties.

3 & 4 Floral Place
7–9 Northampton Grove
London N1 2PL
Tel: 020 7354 4161 (Parent advice line)
email: contact@familyfutures.co.uk
www.familyfutures.co.uk

Family Rights Group (FRG)

A national organisation that advises families who are in contact with social services, about the care of their children.

The Print House, 18 Ashwin Street
London E8 3DL
Tel: 0808 801 0366 (Advice line)
Email: office@frg.org.uk
www.frg.org.uk

Fostering Network

Provides support and information for foster carers to ensure that all children who are fostered receive the highest standards of care.

87 Blackfriars Road, London SE1 8HA
Tel: 020 7620 6400
Email: info@fostering.net
www.fostering.net

Scotland office

2nd Floor, Ingram House
227 Ingram Street, Glasgow G1 1DA
Tel: 0141 204 1400
Email: scotland@fostering.net
www.fostering.net

Wales office

1 Caspian Point
Pierhead Street
Cardiff Bay
Cardiff CF10 4DQ
Tel: 029 2044 0940

Northern Ireland

40 Montgomery Road
Belfast BT6 9HL
Tel: 028 9070 5056

General Register Office for Northern Ireland

Oxford House
49–55 Chichester Street
Belfast BT1 4HL
Tel: 028 9151 3101
www.nidirect.gov.uk/gro

General Social Care Council (GSCC)

Regulatory body for the social care profession in England.

Goldings House, 2 Hay's Lane
London SE1 2HB
Tel: 020 7397 5100
www.gscc.org.uk

Home Education Advisory Service (HEAS)

A UK-based national charity providing information and support for home education. Produces information, provides support for parents, works with LEAs to monitor and inspect home education programmes.

PO Box 98, Welwyn Garden City
Hertfordshire AL8 6AN
Tel: 01707 371 854
email: enquiries@heas.org.uk
www.heas.org.uk

Independent Panel for Special Education Advice (IPSEA)

A charity that aims to ensure that children with special educational needs receive the special education provision to which they are legally entitled. Provides free, independent advice; free advice on appealing to the Special Educational Needs Tribunal (including representation, if needed); second opinions from professionals.

6 Carlow Mews
Woodbridge
Suffolk IP12 1EA
Advice line: 0800 018 4016
Tribunal appeals only: 0845 602 9579
www.ipsea.org.uk

Independent Review Mechanism (IRM)

Reviews adoption and fostering suitability applications from prospective and current carers whose agency has decided not to approve them. Run by BAAF for the Department for Education.

Unit 4, Pavilion Business Park
Royds Hall Road
Wortley
Leeds LS12 6AJ
Tel: 0845 450 3956
www.independentreviewmechanism.org.uk

Independent Review Mechanism (IRM) Cymru

7 Cleeve House
Lambourne Crescent
Cardiff CF14 5GP
Tel: 0845 873 1305
www.irmcymru.org.uk

The Institute for Arts in Therapy and Education

A college of higher education dedicated to in-depth theoretical and practical study of artistic, imaginative and emotional expression and understanding and enhancement of emotional well-being.

2 – 18 Britannia Row, London N1 8PA
Tel: 020 7704 2534
email: info@artspsychotherapy.org
www.artspsychotherapy.org

The Institute for Neuro-phsyiological Psychology

Established in 1975 to research the effects of central nervous system dysfunction on learning difficulties in children and on adults suffering from neuroses. The institute provides detailed information about this topic and about its services on its website or via post.

Warwick House, 1 Stanley Street
Chester CH1 2LR
Tel: 01244 311 414
www.inpp.org.uk

Institute of Child Health

Works in partnership with the Great Ormond Street Hospital to form the largest paediatric training and research centre in the UK. The hospital offers the widest range of paediatric specialists in the country.

30 Guildford Street, London WC1N 1EH
Tel: 020 7242 9789
www.ucl.ac.uk/ich

Intercountry Adoption Centre (IAC)

The only specialist centre for intercountry adoption in the UK, it offers confidential information and advice service for intercountry adopters at any stage of adoption or post adoption. Services include an advice line; counselling for families or for young people who were adopted from overseas; training for professionals involved in adoption; and consultation days for prospective intercountry adopters.

71–73 High Street, Barnet
Hertfordshire EN5 5UR
Tel: 020 8447 4753 (Advice line)
email: info@iaccentre.org.uk
www.iaccentre.org.uk

Jewish Association for Fostering, Adoption and Infertility (JAFA)

10 Fairview Way
Edgware
Middlesex HA8 8JF
Tel: 020 8952 3638

Lesbian and Gay Foster and Adoptive Parents Network

c/o Stonewall Parenting
Tower Building
York Road
London SE1 7NX
Tel: 0800 050 2020
email: info@stonewall.org.uk
www.stonewall.org.uk

The Mental Health Foundation

Provides information and support for people and families who have any type of mental health problem and/or learning disability. Included within the MHF is The Foundation for People with Learning Disabilities.

9th Floor, Sea Containers House
20 Upper Ground
London SE1 9QB
Tel: 020 7803 1100
www.mentalhealth.org.uk

Scotland office

Merchants House
30 George Square, Glasgow G2 1EG
Tel: 0141 572 0145
www.mentalhealth.org.uk

Wales office

Merlin House
1 Langstone Business Park
Priory Drive
Newport NP18 2HJ
Tel: 01633 415434

National Association for Special Educational Needs (NASEN)

Promotes the education, training, advancement and development of people with special educational needs. Services to members include several regular publications, and regional courses and conferences.

4–5 Amber Business Village
Amber Close, Amington
Tamworth B77 4RP
Tel: 01827 311 500
email: welcome@nasen.org.uk
www.nasen.org.uk

National Children's Bureau

Promotes the well-being of children in every aspect of life. Participates in research and policy development, and provides an information service, publications and training.

8 Wakley Street, London EC1V 7QE
Tel: 020 7843 6000
www.ncb.org.uk

Children in Scotland

Tel: 0131 228 8484
Email: info@childreninscotland.org.uk

Children in Wales

Tel: 029 2034 2434
Email: info@childreninwales.org.uk

NORCAP – Adults Affected by Adoption

Provides information, support and counselling services including for those wishing to trace birth relatives.

112 Church Road, Wheatley
Oxfordshire OX33 1LU
Tel: 01865 875 000
email: enquiries@norcap.org.uk
www.norcap.org.uk

National Society for the Prevention of Cruelty to Children (NSPCC)

Provides information and training, in addition to campaign and policy work to prevent abuse of children.

Weston House, 42 Curtain Road
London EC2A 3NH
Helpline: 0808 800 5000
www.nspcc.org.uk

New Family Social

A UK charity for lesbian, gay, bisexual and transgender adopters, foster carers and their children. It provides advice and information, a vibrant messageboard, as well as social events for parents and children to get together.

PO Box 66244
London
E9 9BD
Tel: 0843 289 9457
www.newfamilysocial.co.uk

Office of Public Sector Information (OPSI)

National Archives
102 Petty France
London SW1H 9AJ
Email: legislation@nationalarchives.gsi.gov.uk
www.legislation.gov.uk

Our Place

A registered charity that provides support for families who foster or adopt. Offers workshops, activities, consultations, networking opportunities.

139 Fishponds Road
Eastville, Bristol BS5 6PR
Tel: 0117 951 2433
email: ourplace1@btconnect.com

Overseas Adoption Support and Information Service (OASIS)

A self-help group that provides information and advice for intercountry adopters, as well as post-adoption support. Produces leaflets and a newsletter, operates an advice line and conducts seminars.

www.adoptionoverseas.org

PACE: Project for Advocacy, Counselling and Education

Offers support, information and training for lesbian and gay partners and individuals considering or involved in adoption.

34 Hartham Road
London N7 9JL
Tel: 020 7700 1323
Email: info@pacehealth.org.uk
www.pacehealth.org.uk

Parentline (part of Family Lives)

Confidential helpline provides information and emotional support to parents.

Tel: 0808 800 2222
Textphone: 0800 783 6783
www.familylives.org.uk

Positive Parenting Publications and Programmes

Provides information, resources and training for parents and those who support them.

109 Court Oak Road
Birmingham B17 9AA
Tel: 0845 643 1939
email:info@parenting.org.uk
www.parenting.org.uk

Post-adoption and adoption support services

Please see Section 5 of this handbook.

School Health Service

Identifies and assesses children who have physical, emotional or behavioural problems. It includes a named school nurse and paediatric doctors who have additional training to help with school services. The Health Service provides advice to LEAs and offers specialist services, such as enuresis (bedwetting) clinics, audiology services, and support/advice for families and children with physical and emotional difficulties. Contact your local authority or LEA to find phone numbers for your local School Health Teams.

Scottish Health on the Web (SHOW)

Provided by the NHS in Scotland, this site provides general health information, contact details of all NHS Trusts, and links to other websites.

www.show.scot.nhs.uk

Social, Emotional and Behavioural Difficulties Association (SEBDA)

Promotes services for children and young people who have emotional and behavioural difficulties, and supports professionals working with young people. Produces journal, *Emotional and Behavioural Difficulties*, that provides a variety of articles written mainly by professionals in the field. The journal is available from SAGE Publications.

SEBDA Head office
Room 211
The Triangle
Exchange Square
Manchester M4 3TR
Tel: 0161 240 2418
email: admin@sebda.org
www.sebda.org

Special Education Consortium

See contact details for Council for Disabled Children.

The Stationery Office

Tel: 0870 242 2345
www.tsoshop.co.uk (online shop)

TalkAdoption

A free, confidential national helpline for young people (to 25 years old) who have a link with adoption, whether adoptee, friend or relative.

Tuesday–Friday 3–9 pm
Tel: 0808 808 1234
www.afteradoption.org.uk

The Who Cares? Trust

Promotes services for children and young people in public care and those who have left public care. Publishes 'Who Cares?' magazine quarterly.

Kemp House
152–160 City Road
London EC1V 2NP
Tel: 020 7251 3117
email: mailbox@thewhocarestrust.org.uk
www.thewhocarestrust.org.uk

UK Youth

A network of organisations dedicated to supporting young people to realise their potential. Delivers and supports high-quality voluntary work and informal education for young people. Provides publications for young people and youth workers about emotional/behavioural issues.

7 Heron Quays
Canary Wharf
London E14 4JB
Tel: 020 3137 3814
email: info@ukyouth.org
www.ukyouth.org

United Kingdom Council for Psychotherapy (UKCP)

Holds national register of psychotherapists and gives details of local psychotherapists and counsellors.

2nd Floor, Edward House
2 Wakley Street
London EC1V 7LT
Tel: 020 7014 9955
email:info@ukcp.org.uk
www.ukcp.org.uk

YoungMinds: the children's mental health charity

The national charity committed to improving the mental health of all children and young people. Produces a variety of information about many mental health issues, including 'YoungMinds Magazine'. Provides a consultancy service; works with health, education and social services, and the voluntary sector to develop services for children with mental health problems.

Suite 11, Baden Place
Crosby Row
London SE1 1YW
Tel: 020 7089 5050
www.youngminds.org.uk

YoungMinds Parents' Information Service

A telephone service providing information and advice for anyone with concerns about the mental health of a child or young person.

Helpline: 0808 802 5544
www.youngminds.org.uk/pis

Youth Access

The largest provider of free and confidential youth counselling and information centres throughout the UK. You can find your local service on:
www.youthaccess.org.uk

Appendix 3: National Minimum Standards (NMS) applicable to the provision of adoption services

General Introduction

The National Minimum Standards (NMS) together with the adoption regulations form the basis of the regulatory framework under the Care Standards Act 2000 for the conduct of adoption agencies and adoption support agencies.

The values statement below explains the important principles which underpin these Standards.

Values – children

- The child's welfare, safety and needs are at the centre of the adoption process.

- Adopted children should have an enjoyable childhood, and benefit from excellent parenting and education, enjoying a wide range of opportunities to develop their talents and skills leading to a successful adult life.

- Children are entitled to grow up as part of a loving family that can meet their developmental needs during childhood and beyond.

- Children's wishes and feelings are important and will be actively sought and fully taken into account at all stages of the adoption process.

- Delays should be avoided as they can have a severe impact on the health and development of the children waiting to be adopted.

- A sense of identity is important to a child's well-being. To help children develop this, their ethnic origin, cultural background, religion, language and sexuality need to be properly recognised and positively valued and promoted.

- The particular needs of disabled children and children with complex needs will be fully recognised and taken into account.

- Where a child cannot be cared for in a suitable manner in their own country, intercountry adoption may be considered as an alternative means of providing a permanent family.

- Children, birth parents/guardians and families and adoptive parents and families will be valued and respected.

- A genuine partnership between all those involved in adoption is essential for the NMS to deliver the best outcomes for children; this includes the Government, local government, other statutory agencies, Voluntary Adoption Agencies and Adoption Support Agencies.

Values – adopted adults and birth relatives

- Adoption is an evolving life-long process for all those involved – adopted adults, and birth and adoptive relatives. The fundamental issues raised by adoption may reverberate and resurface at different times and stages throughout an individual's life.

- Adopted people should have access to information and services to enable them to address adoption-related matters throughout their life.

- Agencies have a duty to provide services that considers the welfare of all parties involved and should consider the implications of decisions and actions for everyone involved.

- Agencies should seek to work in partnership with all parties involved, taking account of their views and wishes in decision-making.

- Agencies should acknowledge differences in people's circumstances and establish policies that provide non-discriminatory services.

- Adopted adults have their adoptive identity safeguarded and the right to decide whether to be involved in contact or communication with birth family members.

The detailed standards are the basis for expected outcomes. These outcomes include the following:

- Children know that their views, wishes and feelings are taken into account in all aspects of their care; are helped to understand why it may not be possible to act upon their wishes in all cases; and know how to obtain support and make a complaint.

- Children have a positive self view, emotional resilience and knowledge and understanding of their background.

- Children enjoy sound relationships with their prospective adopters, interact positively with others and behave appropriately.

- Children feel safe and are safe; children understand how to protect themselves and are protected from significant harm including neglect, abuse and accident.

- Children live in a healthy environment where their physical, emotional and psychological health is promoted and where they are able to access the services they need to meet their health needs.

- Children are able to enjoy their interests, develop confidence in their skills and are supported and encouraged to engage in leisure activities.

- The education and achievements of children is actively promoted as valuable in itself and as part of their preparation for adulthood. Children are supported to achieve their educational potential.

- Contact with birth parents, siblings, other members of the birth family and significant others is arranged and maintained when it is beneficial to the child.

- Children live with prospective adopters whose home provides adequate space to a suitable standard. The child enjoys access to a range of activities which promote their development.

- The adoption agency approves adopters who can meet most of the needs of looked after children who are to be placed for adoption and who can provide them with a home where the child will feel loved, safe and secure.

- Children have clear and appropriate information about themselves, their birth parents and families, and life before their adoption.

- Birth parents and birth families take an active part in the planning and implementation of their child's adoption.

- Children benefit from stable placements and are matched and placed with prospective adopters who can meet most, if not all, of their assessed needs.

- Children feel loved, safe and secure with their prospective adoptive parents with whom they were originally placed; and these children were placed within 12 months of the decision of the agency's decision-maker that they should be placed for adoption.

- Children and adults affected by adoption receive an assessment of their adoption support needs.

- Service users confirm that the adoption support services provided met or are meeting their assessed needs.

- Adopted adults and birth relatives are assisted to obtain information in relation to the adoption, where appropriate, and contact is facilitated between an adopted adult and their birth relative if that is what both parties want.

- The adoption panel and decision-maker make timely, quality and appropriate recommendations/decisions in line with the overriding objective to promote the welfare of children throughout their lives.

  Where there are changes, these are noted under the headings in *Effective Panels* with page references. There is a section in

the introduction to the Guidance – para 5, 'Making the adoption process work well' – which is included here, in summary.

Appendix 4:
The Adopters' Charter

The Adopters' Charter was introduced by the Department for Education in November 2011. Its Ministerial Foreword expresses the hope that adoption agencies 'will endorse, implement and build on its principles and that, at the same time, it will give adopters the confidence to question agency planning and decision making'. The Charter is reproduced below.

Children come first

- Adoption is first and foremost a service for children who cannot live with their birth family. Children should be helped to understand what adoption means and supported throughout the adoption journey and beyond.

- Adoption is a life-changing decision that affects the child, and his or her birth and adoptive families. It must be made with the child's best interests, wishes, feelings and needs at its heart and on the basis of sound evidence and high quality assessments.

Adoption agencies must:

- Ensure that children are placed, with siblings wherever possible, within a timescale that is best for them and without unnecessary delay.

- Treat prospective adopters and adopters with openness, fairness and respect.

- Make prospective adopters' first points of contact informative and welcoming.

- Approach adopter recruitment in the spirit of inclusiveness with a view to identifying potential and opportunity – no-one should be automatically excluded.

- Recruit prospective adopters who can meet all or most of the needs of children waiting for, or likely to need, adoption and signpost prospective adopters to other agencies if there is insufficient local demand.

- Explain to prospective adopters the needs and profiles of the children waiting to be adopted.

- Ensure preparation and training, the home study assessment, and approval process are explained and proceed efficiently.

- Regularly review progress on matching with prospective adopters, and inform them about the Adoption Register and refer them to this within required timescales.

- Provide adopters and prospective adopters with information, counselling and support, as and when needed, throughout the adoption journey and beyond.

- Provide prospective adopters with information about the Independent Review Mechanism.

- Work in partnership, and with other agencies and the Courts, to ensure that all decisions are timely and joined-up.

Adoptive parents must:

- Be aware that adoption often brings challenges as well as joy, be realistic about the needs of children awaiting adoption, and accept that with support they may be able to consider adopting a child with a different profile to the child they originally envisaged adopting.

- Make the most of opportunities to develop their parenting skills, and seek support when needed at the earliest stage.

- Do all they can to enable their adopted child to feel loved and secure, and to reach their potential.

Reproduced from *The Adopter's Charter*, Department for Education, 2011.
This information is licensed under the terms of the Open Government Licence (www.dfe.gov.uk/childrenandyoungpeople/families/adoption, accessed 14/11/11).

Index